In this accessible, experiential, and thought-provoking commentary, Brian Borgman provides faithful exegesis, practical application, and balanced perspective on perhaps one of the most misunderstood books of the Bible. Borgman demonstrates that Ecclesiastes is not about life's vanity (lack of purpose) but its vapor (lack of permanence). Although Solomon is realistic about life in a fallen world that is full of uncertainty, injustice, suffering, pain, and death, he also shows that man's vaporous life is full of God's beautiful gifts—like food, youth, work, and marriage—and that we can glorify our Creator by enjoying these gifts with thanksgiving. The good life, then, is one lived *soli Deo gloria*—for the glory of God alone and in the enjoyment of Him alone. Be prepared to have your assumptions about Ecclesiastes transformed!

—Joel R. Beeke
Chancellor and Professor of Homiletics & Systematic Theology
Puritan Reformed Theological Seminary

Get ready to be refreshed, strengthened, steadied, and wisened. Through this commentary, Brian will help you navigate life as it really is. Brian Borgman's commentary on Ecclesiastes is here to deliver the book from a bad reputation and the reader from immaturity. Ecclesiastes has a reputation for being esoteric, disheartening, and confusing. Brian masterfully exposes the true meaning through his treatment of the underlying interpretive grids in the book. This commentary will help you navigate life's ups and downs, gains and losses, sorrows and joys.

— Scott Brown
Pastor at Hope Baptist Church, Wake Forest, NC
President of Church and Family Life

For many people, the book of Ecclesiastes seems just too puzzling and negative to interest them. However, Brian Borgman's exposition of Ecclesiastes will change their minds, because through careful analysis and vivid writing he has explained the positive message of this biblical text in a compelling fashion. Life is indeed short, and it contains a lot of things that we cannot understand or control, yet God has also given us the ability to find joy in our brief and perplexing lives. If you have avoided Ecclesiastes, thinking it depressing and discouraging, let Borgman take you by the hand and show you its delights.

— Daniel Estes
Distinguished Professor of Old Testament
Cedarville University

Discerning the meaning of Ecclesiastes has eluded commentators through the ages. Not Brian Borgman. Through meticulous exegesis and profound pastoral insight, he skillfully unveils the true meaning behind Qoheleth's message. Borgman convincingly demonstrates that Ecclesiastes is anything but "meaningless"; instead, it brims with timeless biblical wisdom applicable to every demographic. *Don't Waste Your Breath* is one book on which your breath will not be wasted! Highly recommended.

—Robert Gonzales
Dean, Reformed Baptist Seminary

I thank God that Brian Borgman not only preached through Ecclesiastes but also reduced his sermons to book form. This exposition of Ecclesiastes is a breath of fresh air. Here are twenty chapters of wisdom gleaned from someone who was stunned by the realization that life was a vapor. Solomon had enough God-inspired wisdom to appreciate the centrality of God as he took a mental journey through this brief and uncertain life. This book will help you to do the same. Enjoy the ride!

—Conrad Mbewe
Pastor of Kabwata Baptist Church
Founding chancellor of the African Christian University in Lusaka, Zambia

Brian takes a fresh positive approach to the book of Ecclesiastes, finding hope in the gospel despite the brevity of this life. This is not a book Brian could have written when he was thirty. He needed to pastor the same congregation for thirty years (marrying and burying), to become a grandfather, and to undergo brain surgery to gain the wise personal insights he offers in this book. This treatment of Ecclesiastes is personal, transparent, readable, carefully researched, and humble. I found this commentary so helpful that I am almost ready to take the plunge and preach from Ecclesiastes for the first time.

—Dr. Jim Newheiser
Professor of Christian Counseling and Pastoral Theology
Director of the Christian Counseling Program
Reformed Theological Seminary, Charlotte
IBCD Executive Director

The biblical book of Ecclesiastes has been variously called "enigmatic," "troublesome," "puzzling," and even "strange," by so many, even those who have actually tried to diligently understand it. Some unbelievers think it is a book so seemingly disturbing and mysterious, that they frankly find it impossible to grasp, finally mocking it altogether. Others do not—those who actually believe in God (whether Jews or Christians)—yet seem rather to just throw up their hands in frustration, confessing ignorance of the book's overall thrust and meaning. If you find yourself somewhere in the middle of this wide spectrum of views, please consider reading this excellent book by Brian Borgman. From my perspective, at least, Dr. Borgman truly understands both the scope and meaning of this biblical book of divine wisdom, which we call *Ecclesiastes*. Through solid English prose and sure-footed biblical interpretation, Borgman leads you by the hand, ably explaining each section of the Scriptural text, thereby helping the reader understand the whole. My thanks indeed, to the author, for a skillful portrayal of life under the sun, and how you and I ought to humbly respond to it.

—Lance Quinn
Vice-President The Expositors Seminary
Jupiter, Florida

In his new commentary on Ecclesiastes, Brian Borgman helpfully unravels much of the difficulty often found in this challenging book of the Bible. Well-written and reliable, this work will benefit any gospel minister with its solid exegesis and Christ-centeredness. This will be among the first resources I pull from my shelf whenever I preach from this book.

—Pastor Rob Ventura
Author of *Expository Outlines & Observations on Romans*
and co-author of *A Portrait of Paul* and *Spiritual Warfare*

Turns out, Ecclesiastes is far more encouraging than we've been led to think. At least, this is what Brian Borgman has concluded, and his case for this conclusion is at one and the same time well-informed, argued persuasively, clearly written, and spiritually enlivening. I finished my reading of his book with my head bowed in renewed gratitude to God for the privilege of yet another day granted by His grace and kindness. I don't want to waste another breath. Enjoy and serve, in humility, trust, and obedience. This is what life truly is about. I'm deeply grateful to Dr. Borgman for this valuable contribution to our understanding of this precious biblical book and for the tremendous encouragement it is to our faith.

—Bruce A. Ware
Professor of Christian Theology
The Southern Baptist Theological Seminary, Louisville, Kentucky

The book of Ecclesiastes does not get the attention it deserves. If you are not familiar with the book, you'll find Brian Borgman an enlightening guide. If you're planning to preach through the book, you'll want his guidance also. A delightful, enriching study on this uniquely important part of our Bible!

—Fred G. Zaspel
Pastor, Reformed Baptist Church, Franconia, PA
Executive Editor, Books at a Glance
Adjunct Professor of Theology, Southern Baptist Theological Seminary
Co-author with Bruce Waltke, *How to Read and Understand the Psalms* (Crossway, 2023).

DON'T WASTE YOUR BREATH

FOREWORD BY PAUL WASHER

"I will never look at the book of Ecclesiastes the same way again."

DON'T WASTE YOUR BREATH

ECCLESIASTES AND THE JOY OF A FLEETING LIFE

BRIAN BORGMAN

FREE
GRACE
PRESS

FREEGRACEPRESS.COM

Don't Waste Your Breath:

Ecclesiastes and the Joy of a Fleeting Life

Published by:

Free Grace Press

Email: support@freegracepress.com
Website: freegracepress.com

Printed in the United States of America

Cover design by Jesse James Dickenson and Scott Schaller

ISBN: 978-1-7338517-5-6

For additional Reformed Baptist titles, please visit our website at freegracepress.com

Dedicated to the sweet memory of
Mateo Giovanni Zeron (2003–2023)
Your life was indeed a vapor,
But it remains a precious gift from God.

A Word About the Dedication

This book is affectionately and appropriately dedicated to the memory of Mateo Zeron. Mateo's family is family to me. I baptized Walter Zeron (Mateo's dad). I officiated Sarah Denton (Mateo's mom) and Walter Zeron's wedding. Over the course of the years, I baptized their daughter, Olivia, and officiated her wedding, baptized their oldest son Sebastian, and on June 5, 2022, I baptized Mateo. Mateo was a sweet kid, who loved the Lord and loved life. Mateo's grandparents, Jeff and Cathy Denton are dear, dear friends. All of them have been faithful members at Grace Community Church for many years. They are more than church members; they are family and friends. In August 2023, Mateo died in an ATV accident on the ranch where he worked. He was only nineteen years old. Mateo encapsulated the message of Ecclesiastes, not only in that his life was a mere breath, but that he enjoyed the short life God had given. With joy and sadness, I dedicate this book to his memory.

ACKNOWLEDGMENTS

This very morning (Oct. 16, 2023), my wife Ariel was by her mother's bedside as she breathed her last. Ariel's mom Dolores turned 85 today. Today we feel the strange weight that life is a mere breath. My wife is a cheerful warrior. She loves and serves better than anybody I know. She encouraged me to keep at Ecclesiastes. I am glad she did. Ariel Joaquina Borgman, I love you.

I want to acknowledge those who helped me make this manuscript better. My fellow elder Daniel Corey helped with chapter and unit titles. He is a gift to me. Carissa Feathers applied her keen eye and fixed my multitude of mistakes. Paul Washer gave me great encouragement and feedback. Thank you, brother, for writing the foreword. My friend Jesse Dickenson worked hard on the cover design. Thanks for your skill.

Jeff Johnson of Free Grace Press is a good friend. Thank you for your enthusiastic acceptance of this book for publication.

For those who offered comments and endorsements, thank you!

To Grace Community Church in Minden, NV, who heard two sermon series on Ecclesiastes (c. 2004 and 2022–23), thank you for your earnest and joyful reception of the Word.

Finally, to my Father who is the sovereign Lord over this brief life and over eternity, I offer my gratitude and praise.

Contents

Foreword

We all recognize that the gospel and the kingdom of Christ have been advanced through the publication of sound literature; however, we must always proceed with caution. Solomon warned that "the writing of many books is endless, and excessive devotion to books is wearying to the body" (Eccl. 12:12). His warning has special application to the contemporary Christian. We live in an age in which the ease of publication has inundated the reader with an excess of books so the library shelves of even the most conscientious bibliophile are filled with more unread volumes that any would care to admit. To add insult to injury, it is equally obvious that we would all do well to spend more time in the only book that is truly indispensable to the Christian faith and the continuation of the church—the inspired, inerrant, and all-sufficient Scriptures (2 Tim. 3:16).

We must hold unwaveringly to the truth that "the Holy Scripture is the only sufficient, certain, and infallible rule of all saving knowledge, faith, and obedience" (1689 LBC, ch.1). However, we must also make use of those works that faithfully expound the Scriptures and give us greater insight into the great doctrines of the faith. Some of these works are multivolume while others are the size of a tract, but the one thing they all have in common is that, instead of drawing the reader away from the Scriptures, they draw them to the Scriptures and help them understand what they are reading. These works function as a Philip to the Ethiopian, who when asked, "Do you understand what you are reading?" replied, "Well, how could I, unless someone guides me? (Acts 8:30–31).

As I read through this work by Dr. Brian Borgman, he played the role of a Philip and enabled me to understand the book of Ecclesiastes in a completely new light. I no longer interpret Solomon's words as the somber musings of a secular sage about the harsh realities of this fallen world. Instead, they have been transformed into a message of hope, a catalyst to trust God, and a goad to live life to the fullest.

As you read through this work, you will be confronted with the realities of life in a fallen world. Yes, there is suffering, pain, death, and oftentimes an encroaching sense of futility. However, for the believer, the brevity of life is an incentive to live life to the fullest, and the uncertainties of life are opportunities to trust in an omnipotent, loving, and faithful Creator who gives good gifts to His children and will one day make all things new. Contemporary Christianity, especially in the West, is filled with extremes. On one hand, there are voices urging believers to live their best life now, almost in disregard of eternity. On the other hand, there are voices admonishing us to put our heads down, look for nothing in this life, and mournfully long for heaven. Dr. Borgman sweeps away both extremes by simply expounding the book of Ecclesiastes. He shows us that we are to relish every good thing as a gift from God, face every hardship with hope in a sovereign God, and await a new heaven and earth with great expectation. I will never look at the book of Ecclesiastes the same way again. After reading this work, I found a renewed freedom, even compulsion, to enjoy all of God's temporal gifts, a clarity and confidence to endure the trials of this fallen age, and lastly, a steadfast hope that does not disappoint. I am greatly indebted. You will be too.

Paul Washer
Founder and Missions Director
HeartCry Missionary Society, 2024

This Misty Moment

My family and I were vacationing on the Oregon coast. These vacations had become our much-anticipated summer ritual. I was standing in the cabin, taking in the sea air, watching my kids play, and feeling a sense of fatherly delight. Then it hit me like an ocean wave. I thought to myself, "There is my daughter. She is about to go to high school. Where did the time go? It seems like yesterday she was crawling on the floor, and wearing Osh-Kosh overalls, and cutely mispronouncing 'macaroni.' Before I know it, she will graduate from college, get married and start having babies!"

I did not realize it then, but that sobering, misty moment would get a name. The emotions, the thoughts, the fear and even the sense of depression would get a name. I was having a *hebel*[1] moment. The moment lingered. The death of my grandparents was still very fresh on my mind, and I thought, "Just as I have watched my dad bury his parents, so my kids are going to watch me bury my parents. It will happen before I know it. But then their kids will watch them bury me!" A wave of melancholy overtook me. "Where has the time gone? I will never get it back. It is past, relegated to photos and fading memories."

---

[1] *Hebel* (pronounced *he-vel*) is a Hebrew word that is often translated "vanity."

As I presently reflect on that moment in the cabin on the Oregon coast, my little girl has been married for over ten years and is the mother of three precious boys. Calvin is now 10, while Sean and Elliott are twins and 8 years old. My children have watched me bury my mother. Again, I ask, "Where has the time gone? Why has it gone by so fast?" On that memorable day, I had an epiphany. I knew that the book of Ecclesiastes would be an important part of navigating through these emotions. For some strange reason, explainable only by the work of divine providence, I knew I had to fulfill a long-standing desire: I needed to get to the bottom of Ecclesiastes. That day on vacation would compel me to complete a journey in the book of Ecclesiastes that had started years before. It would be this journey which would give me a perspective on this experience and a biblical response to that sense of despair. My walk with Solomon would give me a category, called *hebel*, that would help me enjoy the fleeting chapters of life. In fact, my exposition of this very enigmatic, and frequently misunderstood book called "Ecclesiastes" is one of the most liberating things I have ever done as a pastor and one of the most beneficial as a Christian.

The Bible's Problem Child

Ecclesiastes has been called "the black sheep of the Bible."[2] It has been called the "problem child of Scripture."[3] Iain Provan has commented, "Ecclesiastes has a long history of perturbation behind it."[4] And yet for all its bad press, the book has always captured my attention. When I was in college I took an elective on wisdom literature, trying to better understand Scripture's "problem child." When I was in seminary, I took another class that covered Ecclesiastes. Although I was able to grow some in my understanding of the Bible's "black sheep,"

---

[2] J. Stafford Wright, "The Interpretation of Ecclesiastes" in *Reflecting with Solomon: Studies on the Book of Ecclesiastes*, ed. Roy Zuck (Eugene, OR: Wipf & Stock, 2003), 17.

[3] Ronald B. Allen, "Seize the Moment, Meaning in Qohelet," (paper presented at the Northwest Section Meeting of the ETS, April 1988), 1.

[4] Iain Provan, *The NIV Application Commentary: Ecclesiastes, Song of Songs* (Grand Rapids: Zondervan, 2001).

I could not unravel the mystery. I collected articles, books, and commentaries. I read, I asked questions, read more, and still the message of this book eluded me. The mystery of the book is wrapped up in so many of the apparent pessimistic and even contrary statements to what is in the rest of the Bible.

This book was like a jigsaw puzzle to me. Some expositors held up various pieces and claimed to know what the picture on the box was supposed to look like. But those claims always sounded off or incomplete. Was I chasing the wind? In the back of my mind, I wanted to preach Ecclesiastes, but I knew I was not ready. I had not found the corner pieces of the puzzle. I had not discovered the edges. It is a fool's errand to try to put a puzzle together without the corners and edges. I knew I needed to see the forest if I was ever going to understand the trees. My "*hebel* moment" gave me the impetus to put the puzzle together. I was driven.

Life's Like a Puzzle

In the winter following that momentous summer vacation, I took a study leave and headed back to the same cabin in Oregon with my Bible and as many commentaries and articles as possible. Every morning I read Ecclesiastes in one sitting, in different translations, Hebrew Bible close at hand. I spent the rest of the day focused on one aspect of the book. As I started digging, I realized that most of the commentators on Ecclesiastes took a dark and pessimistic view. Although I already had some knowledge of these approaches, they seemed increasingly deficient to me. One study Bible said that this book was man's wisdom; it was wisdom "under the sun." All these views seem to be saying that Ecclesiastes is really nothing more than the best of human wisdom. To be sure, inspiration guarantees that it was accurately recorded, but the conclusions are simply human conclusions. Frankly, this view had no appeal to me. Why not accurately record Confucius or Plato and throw them in too?

---

[5] *Scofield Reference Bible* (New York: Oxford University Press, 1917), 696.

This view seemed to demean the book and make it of no lasting benefit. If the "conclusions and reasonings are, after all, man's"[5] then why preach it?

Other authors argued along similar lines, saying that the message of the book is really without eternal value, except of course the last few verses. Upon such a claim, the authors asked the obvious question, "Why, then, you ask, is it in the Bible at all? The answer is that it is there as a foil, i.e., as a contrast to what the rest of the Bible teaches … it is secular, fatalistic wisdom that a practical (not theoretical) atheism produces."[6] Really? Although I respect the authors of this otherwise helpful book, this view of Ecclesiastes seemed meaningless. Why would God need to devote an entire book in the Bible that has no value other than showing me what practical atheism produces? Isn't that clear enough in many places in the Bible? Isn't that clear enough in life all around us? Ecclesiastes seemed to demand more respect than that. It seemed to be saying something more important.

Another explanation was that there were two authors of this strange book. There was the one who wrote the bulk of it. He was a skeptic and unorthodox in his theology. Then there was the guy who saved the book from the ash-heap who writes a prologue and identifies himself as Solomon (son of David, King in Jerusalem). Claiming to be the son of David for credibility (1:1–11), he then tacked on an orthodox epilogue about fearing God and judgment (12:9–15). This "frame-narrator" (the author who writes a short prologue and epilogue) gives the book its orthodox bookends, with the unorthodox skepticism in between.[7] Again, this interpretation seemed dislocated at best. I was convinced that Ecclesiastes had something far more profound and beneficial to offer the reader.

---

[6] Gordon Fee and Douglas Stuart, *How to Read the Bible for All It's Worth*, 2nd ed. (Grand Rapids: Zondervan, 1993), 2–14.

[7] This is the position of Tremper Longman, *The Book of Ecclesiastes*, The New International Commentary on the Old Testament (Grand Rapids: Eerdmans, 1997). Longman and Dan Allender popularized the view in *Breaking the Idols of Your Heart* (Downers Grove, IL: Zondervan, 2007). See my review of *Breaking the Idols of Your Heart* in *The Southern Baptist Theological Journal*, 12.1 (2008), 116–18, for an assessment.

The views I had been exposed to earlier in college revolve around the writer of Ecclesiastes having some internal debate with himself or with a make-believe opponent. Many took the view that there was a "life under the sun/without God" vs. "life above the sun/with God" battle going on. The battle was to show how meaningless a secular life really is. For instance, "Ecclesiastes was written to depress us into dependence on our joyous God and his blessed will for our lives. If we are attempting to live the 'meaningful' secular life—a life 'under the sun' without reference to God—we are attempting to grasp the unattainable. We are 'striving after the wind.' The only remedy to meaninglessness and depression caused by grief by a godless life is God."[8] In the end, according to this common view, Ecclesiastes is an evangelistic tract to depress people into faith in God.

Others said the author was having a "faith vs. reason" dialogue. This dialectical approach was common enough, but in the end also unconvincing.[9] Trying to determine which statements fit into what category seemed arbitrary. These views were unpersuasive to me. It seemed like holding up random pieces of the puzzle and saying, "This piece is what it is all about." Or holding up two pieces that looked opposite of each other and saying, "This is how they fit together," smashing the pieces together to make them fit. I came to realize that all these negative, pessimistic views of Ecclesiastes were all based on the assumption that the word *hebel* (used in 1:2 and a total of thirty-eight times in the book) meant "vanity," or "meaningless," or "futility."

Ultimately, no matter what view was presented, it posited an overall negative message rooted in the idea that "everything is vanity." As Daniel Fredericks notes, "According to the consensus of interpretation, regardless of the number of diversified

---

[8] Doug O'Donnell, "Ecclesiastes Notes," in *Gospel Transformation Study Bible*, ed. Bryan Chappell (Wheaton, IL: Crossway, 2018), 938, n. 1:14.

[9] "Dialectical" refers to a discussion or argument based on contradictory ideas. Here, "faith vs. reason" are the two contradictory ideas.

approaches, *everything is vanity or meaningless.*"[10] I have come to see, with the help of a small but growing handful of others, that this assumption unnecessarily darkens the book. I have also come to see that this view of *hebel* is not accurate. My journey in Ecclesiastes has led me to believe that this is a wonderful, even positive book that shows us that life is a gift from God which is to be enjoyed for His glory. *Hebel* is not meaninglessness, it is vapor, breath, or mist (as I will demonstrate). Ecclesiastes wrestles with the brevity of life, not its meaninglessness.

An Indiana Jones Adventure Ride

When my kids were little, we went to Disneyland, and they begged us to ride on the Indiana Jones Adventure. The ride starts out with a jolt, jerks you left and then right, gradually goes up, suddenly goes down, then unpredictably and abruptly, indeed, violently, turns right then right again. Then it ends with a bone-jarring and sudden stop. That is Ecclesiastes! It is a ride of unexpected twists and turns, abrupt stops and starts that rattles the passenger and violently herniates the discs in his back with the unexpected. I trust that you will stick it out with me. It is worth every bit of the jarring, bumpy ride.

Ecclesiastes is an explosive book. David Gibson observes, "It's a book in the Bible that gets under the radar of our thinking and acts like an incendiary device to explode our make-believe games and jolts us into realizing that everything is not as clean and tidy as the 'let's-pretend' world suggests."[11] The "Preacher" of Ecclesiastes is subversive. His is a book that exposes and explodes our illusions and make-believe-life. Ian Provan drives this point home hard: "The 'difficulty' may be that the book speaks truly about reality while we are devoted to illusions.

---

[10] Daniel C. Fredericks, "Ecclesiastes," in *Ecclesiastes and The Song of Songs*, vol. 16 of *Apollos Old Testament Commentary*, ed. David W. Baker and Gordon J. Wenham (Downers Grove, IL: InterVarsity Press, 2010), 42, italics added.

[11] David Gibson, *Living Life Backwards: How Ecclesiastes Teaches Us to Live in Light of the End* (Wheaton, IL: Crossway, 2017), 19.

The 'difficulty' may be that we are not too keen to embrace the truth but prefer to embrace half-truths or lies."[12]

In the pages that follow I want to introduce you to this magnificent, life-changing book. I would also like to point out the corners and edges of this jigsaw puzzle, by showing you the meaning and significance of the key words and phrases like *hebel* (traditionally translated, "vanity"), "under the sun," and "chasing the wind." It would be my pleasure to lead you on a journey through the book, section by section, putting the pieces of the puzzle together. If God should help us, I would also take great joy in showing you that Ecclesiastes is a book about enjoying life even though it is a mere breath. It is a book about trusting the Giver and enjoying His marvelous gifts in this short and often mysterious life. It is a book that shouts at us, "Do not waste your breath (vapor)! Enjoy it while you have it."

There I was, in the living room of that cabin on the Oregon coast. My *hebel* moment would change my life. It was a rough ride, but through God's grace I learned that those years, which seem like days, were not to be mourned because they were over. They were to be celebrated as God's gift to me in this short life. Those years were a breath. Indeed, life is a breath. Life is a series of breaths which one cannot grasp, hold on to, let alone figure out. There is mystery in the breath, but there is a gift in the breath also. I found out it was easy to ruin the gift. If I tried to hang on to it longer than God gave it, I would ruin it. If I tried to get more out of it than God intended, then I would ruin it. But if I could see it for what it was, the gift of a breath on a cold morning, then I could enjoy it as God's gift to me. I thank God for that *hebel* moment. Ecclesiastes became an unexpected source of joy in the mist.

Brian S. Borgman

---

[12] Provan, *Ecclesiastes, Song of Songs*, 25.

1

You're So Vain
(You Probably Thought
This Chapter Was about You)

Neither Vain nor Meaningless

The majority report on Ecclesiastes is that it presents a pessimistic outlook on life. Many commentators and pastors take a view of Ecclesiastes that says the book teaches that life has no ultimate value, or that it promotes a view of life that is secular, even fatalistic. Some reading the NIV are disposed to think the book was written to depress us with "Meaningless! Meaningless! Utterly meaningless! Everything is meaningless." Then according to the majority report, that depression could be used to turn us to God. This is an apparent evangelistic strategy to lead us to emptiness and then to seek God. In one form or another, this is how Ecclesiastes has often been understood and taught. But there is a fatal flaw.

The most crucial aspect to understanding Ecclesiastes and how it connects with our life is to properly grasp the word which our translations translate "vanity," "futility," or "meaningless."

> "Vanity of vanities," says the Preacher, "Vanity of vanities! All is vanity." (Eccl. 1:2 NASB 95, ESV)

> "Absolute futility," says the Teacher. "Absolute

futility. Everything is futile." (Eccl. 1:2 CSB, NET)
Utter futility!—said Koheleth—Utter futility! All
is futile! (Eccl. 1:2 TNK)

"Meaningless! Meaningless!" says the Teacher.
"Utterly meaningless! Everything is meaningless."
(Eccl. 1:2 NIV, NLT)

With all these translations saying basically the same thing, do
we really need to look further? I think we do (and I am not alone
in that assessment).[13] The Hebrew word translated "vanity" is
hebel. It is used 38 times in this book, which is about half of
all Old Testament uses. But when we consider that Solomon
says twice, "*Hebel of hebels. Hebel of hebels. Everything is hebel,*" then
we have a keyword and a key theme that helps us understand
this book.

Not only is this phrase at the beginning of the book (1:2), but it
is also at the end of the book (12:8). The phrase forms bookends
for the readers. This gives us a good indication that the phrase is
the theme which encompasses the whole book. But we should also
take note that the bookend statement is superlative, repetitive,
and comprehensive.

By "superlative," I mean that *hebel of hebels* is a biblical way
of emphasizing something in the highest degree. If we say,
"King of kings," we mean, "the King who is the ultimate king
and over every other king." The thematic verse in Ecclesiastes
emphasizes, therefore, the superlative nature of *hebel,* that is, *hebel*
is a quality in life that surpasses all others. The hint of frustration
or exasperation is also present in this superlative formula.

---

[13] For another dissenting opinion, consider T. D. Gledhill's words: "In Ecclesiastes,
we are faced with a number of difficulties in interpreting the *hebel* concept... Dis-
agreement over these matters leads to a wide variety of interpretative glosses for the
hebel concept: vanity, meaningless, irrational, absurd, illogical, transitory, ephemeral,
illusory, incomprehensible. But we should be careful not to import our 20th-century
existentialism and nihilism into the biblical text. These were not options among the
world views available to Qoheleth, the author of Ecclesiastes. Absurdity and meaninglessness at the heart of the universe are incompatible with biblical theism." T. D.
Gledhill, "Vanity," in *New Dictionary of Biblical Theology,* ed. T. Desmond Alexander and
Brian S. Rosner, electronic ed. (Downers Grove, IL: InterVarsity Press, 2000), 830.

The emphasis continues when Solomon repeats the phrase. In Hebrew, repetition is a way to emphasize something. We use bold or italics; the Hebrews often used repetition. Solomon therefore repeats the superlative phrase and then implicates everything, not just some things, as *hebel*. This leads us to the comprehensive statement: "Everything is *hebel*." The drama and energy of this opening phrase is gripping. In the case of Ecclesiastes, the crescendo comes at the beginning and the end!

We now understand that everything is *hebel* of *hebels*, but what does it mean? Its importance cannot be exaggerated. Its significance demands that we get the meaning of the word right. Old Testament scholar Daniel Fredericks says, "The history of interpretation of Ecclesiastes … is a history mainly of the meaning of *hebel*."[14] In other words, if *hebel* is mistranslated then the whole book is misunderstood. It is like trying to put the jigsaw puzzle together and having the corners and edges from the wrong puzzle! Imagine having a puzzle with a beautiful desert scene. There are cacti, rocks, sand, purple sage, blue sky, and more rocks. But as you look at the corners and edges, they look more like rolling green hills, maybe from Scotland. No wonder the pieces have such a hard time fitting together!

Tracing Out the Temporary

To be fair, most translators are following the lead of a long tradition. The lead came from what is called the Septuagint (LXX), which was the Greek translation of the Hebrew Scriptures. When they got to the word *hebel*, they translated it with *mataiotēs*, a word that can mean "empty."[15] From there, Jerome (342–347 AD) translated the LXX into Latin, in the version

---

[14] Fredericks, "Ecclesiastes," 46.

[15] The Greek word is *mataiotēs*. It is interesting to note that BDAG defines the word as a "state of being without use or value, emptiness, futility, purposelessness, transitoriness" Walter Bauer et al., eds., *A Greek-English Lexicon of the New Testament and Other Early Christian Literature* (Chicago: University of Chicago Press, 2000), 621. Notice, even this Greek word has within its range the possible meaning, "transitory."

known as the Vulgate. He translated the Greek word, *mataiotēs*, with the Latin word *vanitas*, from which we get "vanity."[16]

Walter Kaiser has pointed out, however, that not all Greek translations of the Old Testament followed suit. He cites three other Greek translations which chose a different Greek word for *hebel*. They chose the word *atmis*, translated "breath" or "vapor."[17] It is the word used in James 4:14: "Yet you do not know what tomorrow will bring. What is your life? For you are *a mist* that appears for a little time and then vanishes."[18] So the question is what does *hebel* mean in the Old Testament? Or to ask another question, does the Bible teach that our lives are meaningless? Or does it teach that our lives are a breath or a vapor?

One of the first things to observe is that Abel's name is the Hebrew word *hebel*, depicting the brevity of his life. The word is used in many contexts and, according to the way words work, may have a variety of implications. The basic sense of *hebel* is breath, mist, fog, or vapor.[19] Idols are often described as *hebel* ("vain idols"). But the idea is probably that idols are a vapor, in that they have no substance, no permanence, no real glory. God is a God of glory, that is, He is weighty.[20] But the idols are a mere breath and are insubstantial.[21] Other uses would include

---

[16] Provan says, citing G.A. Barton, "Jerome interprets Ecclesiastes as a treatise aiming 'to show the utter vanity of every sublunary enjoyment, and hence the necessity of betaking one's self to an *ascetic life* devoted entirely to the service of God.'" See Provan, *Ecclesiastes, Song of Songs*, 25, italics added.

[17] *Atmis* is used by Aquila, Theodotion, and Symmachus in their Greek translations. See Kaiser, *Coping with Change*, 58–59.

[18] Of course, the italics are added to this biblical text and not original. Each time there is italics in a quotation of the Bible in this book, it is because they were added. Also, in place of "a mist," the NASB has "a vapor" and the NET has "a puff of smoke."

[19] *New International Dictionary of Old Testament Theology and Exegesis*, Vol 1 (Zondervan, 1997), 1003.

[20] The Hebrew word for weight is *kavod*. "The basic meaning is 'to be heavy, weighty....' From this figurative usage it is an easy step to the concept of a 'weighty' person in society, someone who is honorable, impressive, worthy of respect." John N. Oswalt, "943 כָּבֵד," in *Theological Wordbook of the Old Testament*, ed. R. Laird Harris, Gleason L. Archer Jr., and Bruce K. Waltke (Chicago: Moody Press, 1999), 426.

[21] Two texts that speak of idols as being mere breath or insubstantial are Jeremiah 2:5 and 10:3.

"words," which are said to be *hebel* and are thus translated as "empty words" or "vain words." However, I suggest that it would be better to translate the phrase as "vaporous words," indicating they lack substance or weight. Most often *hebel* is used to describe a mist, a breath, a vapor, or something brief, transient. To underscore this, *hebel* is often coupled with "shadow" denoting that which is passing, fleeting, or transitory.[22]

> I waste away; I will not live forever.
> Leave me alone, for my days are *but* a *breath.*
> *(Job 7:16, see also verse 6)*

> Behold, you have made my days *as* handbreadths,
> And my lifetime as nothing in your sight;
> Surely every man at his best is a mere *breath.*
> Selah.

> Surely every man walks about as a phantom;
> Surely they make an uproar for *nothing;*[23]
> He amasses *riches*, and does not know who will gather them. *(Ps. 39:5–6)*

> With reproofs You chasten a man for iniquity;
> You consume as a moth what is precious to him;
> Surely every man is a mere *breath.* Selah.
> *(Ps. 39:11 NASB 95)*

> Men are nothing but a mere *breath;*
> human beings are unreliable.
> When they are weighed in the scales, all of them together are lighter than air. *(Ps. 62:9 NET)*

> Man is like a mere *breath;*
> His days are like a passing shadow.
> *(Ps. 144:4 NASB 95)*[24]

---

[22] Fredericks, "Ecclesiastes," 28.

[23] "Every human being that walks only a shadow; *a mere puff of wind* is the wealth stored away—no knowing who will profit from it" (Ps. 39:6 NJB).

[24] There are other passages which speak of man's transience without using the word *hebel*. For instance, Psalm 90:5–6, 10, 12. See also Job 7:6–7; James 4:14.

Once we begin to read Ecclesiastes and replace "vanity" with "vapor" or an appropriate synonym, then we understand that the book of Ecclesiastes is not wrestling with the apparent meaninglessness of life, but rather, with the brevity of life and all the pain and mystery that brevity brings. This view of *hebel* is not a novel or fringe view. Fredericks comments that "the view that *hebel* means transience or vapor is gaining traction."[25]

Based on the above understanding of *hebel*, it becomes apparent that Ecclesiastes should read: "Breath of breaths. Breath of breaths. Everything is breath." Or, "Vapor of vapors. Vapor of vapors. Everything is vapor." Or as David Gibson suggests, "The merest of breaths ... the merest of breaths. Everything is a breath."[26]

Kathleen Farmer states the importance of this point:

> It is possible, then, that hebel (meaning a puff of air) might be understood in either a positive or a negative sense. If the translation preserves the metaphor, the reader is forced to decide in what sense the comparison should be taken. In my opinion it is unfortunate that many modern versions of Ecclesiastes have chosen to take the decision away from the reader. Most translators obscure the metaphorical nature of the original statement and replace the concrete, nonjudgmental phrase ("breath" or "puff of air") with various abstract terms—all of which have decidedly negative connotations in English. Even if a case could be made for replacing a metaphor with an adjective or a descriptive phrase, there are legitimate grounds for challenging the negative connotations of the words which many modern translators use to translate hebel in Ecclesiastes.[27]

---

[25] Fredericks, "Ecclesiastes," 52.

[26] Gibson, *Living Life Backwards*, 20.

[27] Kathleen Farmer, *Proverbs and Ecclesiastes: Who Knows What Is Good?* International Theological Commentary (Grand Rapids: Eerdmans, 1991), 143.

As we go through this breath-taking book, we will see that the way Solomon uses *hebel* and the words he frequently pairs with it, indicate not that life is useless, vain, or meaningless, but that it is temporary or transient. Death is certain. This brings some mystery and enigma to life, especially in light of God's permanence. Solomon is wrestling with the pain of a labor-filled life that is a mere breath. Why is this life so short? Why does it go by so fast?

Now for a few observations on *hebel* in Ecclesiastes.

Hebel Is for Everybody

Hebel is a constant in everyone's life. The life of the sinner and the life of the saint are both marked by *hebel*. Nobody escapes it. It is a reality for those who love God and those who hate Him. There is no escaping it. Life is short and elusive, for everyone. Barry Webb noted, "Belief in God does not relieve the observed and experienced fact of *hebel*."[28] So faith does not make the fog of *hebel* go away. The point of the book is not how to get around *hebel*, but how to cope with it and thrive within it.

Hebel Is from God

Hebel is not only a constant for everyone, but also the constant condition of this present life because of God's judgment. *Hebel* is part of the curse. It is the graffiti written all over a fallen world. Therefore, God is the one who is in control of *hebel*. Instead of being an accident, *hebel* is under God's sovereign control as a condition of judgment. As we experience *hebel*, we experience the frustration of a short life. But Solomon will point us not to meaninglessness, but to God who is worthy to be feared and trusted in the mist. God is not transient. He is eternal. As we have our *hebel* moments, we need to see that life's sad chapters, the disappointing chapters, and happy chapters,

---

[28] Barry Webb, *Five Festal Garments: Christian Reflections on The Song of Songs, Ruth, Lamentations, Ecclesiastes, and Esther*, New Studies in Biblical Theology (Downers Grove, IL: InterVarsity Press, 2000), 96.

are all short chapters in a short life in a fallen world. We also need to see that not only is this short life elusive, but also that we are not in the driver's seat. Finally, what makes *hebel* painful is what brings the breath to an end, namely, death.

Hebel and Life Under the Sun

The phrase "under the sun" is used twenty-nine times in Ecclesiastes. It is frequently paired with *hebel*.[29] Many commentators take the phrase to be an expression of life without God. The reality is that "under the sun" is just life. It is life for everybody. Every mere mortal lives "under the sun." It is the perspective, as one writer put it, of our death row cell existence.[30] There is even an assumption about God in the phrase "under the sun," and it is that God is King and Judge in heaven. As Ecclesiastes 5:2 says, "God is in heaven, and you are on earth." As long as we live this life, we experience a fleeting (vaporous) existence "under the sun." Whether life is good, whether it is painful, whether it is lived with wisdom or with folly, it is life under the sun. Life under the sun is just life.

Hebel and Chasing After the Wind

The phrase "striving after the wind" is used seven times, and six of those are paired with *hebel*. Chasing the wind, or shepherding the wind, is trying to do something impossible. It is trying to control the uncontrollable. The wind is constantly changing and unpredictable.

This vapor-like life is marked by the ever-changing winds. A vapor in the wind doesn't stand a chance. For those who think they have their future wrapped up with a neat bow, for those who have done everything right and made all the proper preparations for a life of joy, know this: the wind can shift.

---

[29] For instances of "under the sun" paired with "*hebel*," see Ecclesiastes 1:14; 2:11, 17, 19; 4:7; 5:12; 9:9 (x 2).

[30] M. M. Kline, "Is *Qoheleth* Unorthodox?" review of *The Book of Ecclesiastes*, by Tremper Longman III. *Kerux: A Journal of Biblical Theology*, N. D. https://kerux.com/doc/1303R1.asp.

No one can shepherd the wind. Making plans is wise, but in a life that is a breath on a cold morning, you never know what awaits you at the next turn. This short life is unpredictable and uncontrollable.

There are other key words and phrases in Ecclesiastes, such as, "labor," "profit," "good," "gift," "reward," and derivatives of "joy." All of these will be taken up in due time. What we need to see now is that lack of permanence, rather than meaninglessness, is the message of Ecclesiastes. Brevity, not vanity, is the message. If the goal of Ecclesiastes was to depress us into conversion by presenting an unbelieving worldview or tell us how meaningless life is, then I doubt that at the end of the book it could be said, "The Preacher (Qoheleth) sought to find delightful words and to write words of truth correctly" (Eccl. 12:10). Rather, the book deals with the pain and frustration of a fleeting life that invariably ends in death. It is a book that deals with life and death, and life is always complex. Life is always messy. Therefore, why not have a book that is also complex and messy in dealing with real life and the unwanted intruder, death?

Conclusion

Ecclesiastes stands out in our Bibles as an unusual gift. It is a book of inspired wisdom that sounds different from other books. It deals with the exceptions and mysteries of life. Ecclesiastes helps us break through the make-believe, pretend views of life, which are designed to anesthetize us. If we live anesthetized, fabricated lives, we will be unprepared when it is time to die. Ecclesiastes shouts, "Life is a gift, it is really short, you will die, and you need my wisdom to live it joyfully." Ecclesiastes is an unexpected source of joy that warns us and equips us to not waste our breath before it ends in death.

My wife still uses a little pocket calendar. She is a meticulous planner. One day she sat there looking at her calendar and said, "You know, you write some event down, months ahead of time. You look forward to it. You see it every time you open the calendar and anticipate it. The event comes and goes. It's over. And all you have left are memories and some pictures. It is strange. It is sad. All that anticipation, and then it is over so fast." That is what Ecclesiastes wants you to feel. Ecclesiastes will never be a gift to us unless we feel that sadness first.

2

Life on the Merry-go-round
(1:1-18)

Introduction: Do It Again!

One of the great things about kids is that they are full of wonder. Everything is new. One of the most endearing phrases from these inquisitive little people is, "Do it again!" No matter what it is, peek-a-boo, snapping your fingers, swinging them by their arms in circles until they throw up!—it is all an amazement to them. "Do it again!" The adult always gives up before the child and then tries to create diversions to get off the endless "do it again" merry-go-round.

One of the sad things about being an adult is that we are low on wonder, and everything seems to get old. One of the wearying phrases of life comes from the little ones, "Do it again!" The amazement, for adults, has dwindled, and spinning in circles until you get motion sickness just isn't fun anymore. "Do it again" is just another word for boredom and monotony. Something inside of us says we should have joy and wonder, but we know it has faded.

Ecclesiastes is going to exploit the "do it again" monotony of life, which seems to exacerbate the brevity of life. Ecclesiastes is taking us on a ride. It is a bumpy ride, designed to bang your head against the side window and make you say, "Ouch."

He wants to put a pit in your stomach as you think hard aboutthe things of life that frustrate, bewilder, and even depress us. But he is a faithful guide; he knows where he is taking us. He is a skilled guide; he knows how to make the most out of the ride. So, hang on.

The Laundry of Life (1:1–11)

[1] The words of the Preacher, the son of David,
king in Jerusalem.

[2] Vanity of vanities, says the Preacher,
vanity of vanities! All is vanity.

[3] What does man gain by all the toil
at which he toils under the sun?

[4] A generation goes, and a generation comes,
but the earth remains forever.

[5] The sun rises, and the sun goes down,
and hastens to the place where it rises.

[6] The wind blows to the south
and goes around to the north;
around and around goes the wind,
and on its circuits the wind returns.

[7] All streams run to the sea,
but the sea is not full;
to the place where the streams flow,
there they flow again.

[8] All things are full of weariness;
a man cannot utter it;
the eye is not satisfied with seeing,
nor the ear filled with hearing.

[9] What has been is what will be,
and what has been done is what will be done,
and there is nothing new under the sun.

[10] Is there a thing of which it is said,

"See, this is new"?
It has been already
in the ages before us.

[11] There is no remembrance of former things,
nor will there be any remembrance
of later things yet to be
among those who come after.[31]

The author identifies himself in 1:1: "The words of the Preacher, the son of David, king in Jerusalem." He says again in 1:12, "I the Preacher have been king over Israel in Jerusalem." Many conservative scholars believe Solomon wrote Ecclesiastes and with good reason. The book was written during a monarchy. Daniel Fredericks has demonstrated verbal parallels with Proverbs, Song of Songs, and Solomonic history.[32] Solomonic authorship has also been ably defended by Gleason Archer.[33] The early consensus among Jewish and Christian scholars was that Ecclesiastes expressed Solomon's meditations and reflections in his old age. The book certainly has the flavor of life's twilight. Walt Kaiser further adds, "There is in the book an air of repentance and humility for past values and performance."[34] Ecclesiastes is the thoughts, observations, and reflections of Solomon, in later life, hopefully from the posture of repentance.

But what shall we call him? "The Preacher"? This is the most common among our translations. But others have opted for "the Teacher." It is important to note that the title of the book in Hebrew is also the title of the one speaking, *Qoheleth*.[35]

---

[31] All Scripture is quoted from the English Standard Version (Wheaton, IL: Crossway, 2011), unless otherwise noted.

[32] Fredericks, "Ecclesiastes," 35–36.

[33] Gleason Archer, *A Survey of Old Testament Introduction*, rev. ed. (Chicago: Moody Press, 1974), 478–488. John D. Currid (*Ecclesiastes: A Quest for Meaning* [Leyland, England: Evangelical, 2016], 8) notes, "Many scholars disagree with Solomonic authorship of Ecclesiastes. However, I would suggest that it is fully corroborated by numerous allusions in the text which coincide with specific events and cultural conditions in Solomon's life."

[34] Walter Kaiser, *Ecclesiastes: Total Life* (Chicago: Moody Press, 1979), 31.

[35] Qoheleth is pronounced as *kō-hel-et*.

The name comes from the Hebrew verb qahal, meaning assemble or congregate. The form in Ecclesiastes is a participle meaning the speaker is one who calls an assembly. The problem is that no single term in English seems to do justice to "Qoheleth." "The Preacher" has a church connotation. "The Teacher" denotes the academy, as does "The Professor." Some have suggested, "The Arguer" or "Debater," but that implies a skeptic. My fellow Pastor, Daniel Corey, has creatively suggested, "The Provocateur." It is true, but probably won't catch on!

For this exposition, we will retain Qoheleth when referring to the author (although "Solomon" will sometimes be used as well).[36] Qoheleth is the Shepherd-King-Sage (12:9–11), who is giving a speech. We should view Ecclesiastes not primarily as literature, but as a speech, a sermon, a lecture, reflections, analyses, and at times provocation.

The theme of the book (1:2), "Breath of breaths, breath of breaths, everything is merely breath," is superlative, emphatic, and comprehensive. By repeating the statement at the end of the book (12:8), he underscores the totality of *hebel* as he forms bookends that frame the whole. This is the theme, and it is a painful one. Life is a vapor, it is mist, it is transitory, and painfully brief. Qoheleth then asks the programmatic question of the book, "What does man gain by all the toil at which he toils under the sun?" (1:3). This question in many ways shapes the book and is developed throughout. The question, "What does a man gain?" sets the agenda. What remains after all our hard work? The question is not really about the meaning of life, but rather what is the benefit of hard work. The brevity of life demands the question and begs for an answer. If life is so short and it is filled with toil, what is left over? What is the benefit? The answer will appear to be, at first, "there is no benefit!" But that will not be Qoheleth's final answer.

The question itself, "What advantage or benefit or profit does a man have in all his work?" is not a philosophical question,

---

[36] The New Jerusalem Bible and the Tanakh retain "Qoheleth."

but rather it is a practical one. It is focused on the reality that in this vaporous life we labor and then ask, "will it last?" Again, we ask, "Did it matter?" These questions are based on the dignity of labor (Gen. 2:15–17) and the curse (Gen. 3:17–19). Why spend a life toiling away when it is so short and nothing we do appears to last? Doesn't the curse and the reality of *hebel* nullify any advantage in our labor? This life of labor under the sun seems like building sandcastles. We work, and work, and work. Then comes a wave! "How long do sandcastles last? And how much control do we have over the castle we have constructed? We build for a short time only, and always subject to forces beyond our control. That is what our lives are like."[37]

While we are toiling, we feel like we are accomplishing something, that we are in control. But it is an illusion. The next wave proves it.

Qoheleth wants that to lie heavy on us for a while. He won't give an easy answer. He wants us to feel his pain. To twist the knife a little deeper, he gives us a poem about the cyclical nature of this world. Nature is teaching us something.

Never Full, Never Tired

"A generation goes, and a generation comes, but the earth remains forever" (Eccl. 1:4). Indeed, the transient nature of life is contrasted with the permanence of God's work in creation. When this reality falls on us, it falls on us hard. As one Christian woman told me after the death of her sister-in-law, "One day I will die, and the sun will still rise the next day, and the sky will still be blue, and those who are left behind will be asking the same questions I am asking myself today." The world doesn't skip a beat when a generation goes, or when a generation comes. It does not stop taking note, let alone celebrate. Isaac Watts captured this thought:

> The busy tribes of flesh and blood
> With all their lives and cares,

---

[37] Gibson, *Living Life Backwards*, 21–22.

Are carried downward by your flood,
And lost in foll'wing years.
Time, like an ever-rolling stream,
Bears all its sons away;
They fly forgotten, as a dream
Dies at the op'ning day.[38]

The next few verses talk about the sun, the wind, and rivers. "The sun rises, and the sun goes down, and hastens to the place where it rises" (1:5). Nature appears to be in a hurry to perform its cyclical processes. The sun comes up, goes down, and then runs back to do it all over again. The wind and the streams all follow suit. Nature hears, "Do it again!" and gladly complies. The rhythmic cadence of doing it again and again seems like man in his toil, except for one major difference. The repetitive cycles of nature reflect a stability and permanence that is very unlike our lives. Nature reflects God's permanence and accentuates our impermanence. The sun will rise the day after I die. The wind will still blow, even as my loved ones are gathered at my grave.

Qoheleth registers his complaint. Despite the apparent permanence of the earth and her labors, there is a weariness to it that mocks the monotony of our labor. "All things[39] are full of weariness."[40] The next three verses probably run parallel to the picture of nature (1:9–11). Speaking, seeing, and hearing are done over and over, like the sun rising, the wind blowing, and the streams flowing. But what we say, see, and hear cannot be kept on reserve; it cannot be stored away. What is the point? What does it matter? Our sights, our sounds, and yes, our words, are *hebel*.

---

[38] Isaac Watts, "Our God Our Help in Ages Past," https://www.poetryfoundation.org/poems/50583/our-god-our-help.

[39] "All things" (*kol hadebarim*) can also be translated from the Hebrew as "all of the words."

[40] For the translational difficulties of this verse, see Duane A. Garrett, *Proverbs, Ecclesiastes, Song of Songs, vol. 14 of The New American Commentary* (Nashville: Broadman & Holman, 1993), 285.

Nothing New Under the Sun

Some take verses 9–10 as an explanation of verse 8. "What has been is what will be, and what has been done is what will be done, and there is nothing new under the sun. Is there a thing of which it is said, 'See, this is new?' It has been already in the ages before us."

Human life and history go on and on like endless reruns. Life is like doing laundry. You wash the clothes. You dry the clothes. You fold the clothes. You put away the clothes. They end up in the laundry room a day later only to undergo the same monotonous process. Life is like changing diapers. It is like mowing your lawn. Furthermore, there is nothing new under the sun. Life itself reflects the laborious, ceaseless cycles. It is one puff of breath after another, each one like the one before. And no one can say about any part of it, "Look! This is new!" The antagonist says, "There is new stuff all the time!" Qoheleth says, "Not really." The antagonist says, "Well what about the internet, what about smart phones, what about technology?" Qoheleth laughs. "You think that is new? Let me tell you, all that stuff just moves information faster, but it is still just information. It entertains faster, but it is still just entertainment. By the way," he says with a smirk, "have all those new gadgets made your life better? Have they mitigated the pain of *hebel*? No, they have not. The real story is that for all your gadgets, you are less satisfied and can't wait for the new iPhone to come out." Gibson remarks, "What is new is not really new, and what feels new will soon feel old."[41] The "new" just accentuates and accelerates *hebel*. There is nothing new under the sun.

To add insult to injury, Qoheleth then tells us, "There is no remembrance of former things, nor will there be any remembrance of later things yet to be among those who come after" (1:11). This ride is ruthless! As my wife said, "All you have left is memories and pictures." Our good days, our achievements, our work, even our name, nobody will remember.

---

[41] Gibson, *Living Life Backwards*, 30.

"Well, what if they name a street after me?" Nobody will know who the guy is whose name is on a street sign. Your name just becomes an automated voice on a GPS: "Turn left on Borgman Blvd." Nobody will care. Qoheleth is brutally honest.

Hebel of *hebels*, all is *hebel*. Qoheleth is not going to relieve the tension yet. It will get worse before it gets better. He is not holding an antidote behind his back, waiting for us to shed enough tears. Qoheleth, in due time, will give us a perspective that will empower us to cope with a short life that is consumed with toil. Before he gets there, he insists on a little more analysis.

Chasing After the Wind (1:12–18)

> [12] I the Preacher have been king over Israel in Jerusalem.
>
> [13] And I applied my heart to seek and to search out by wisdom all that is done under heaven. It is an unhappy business that God has given to the children of man to be busy with.
>
> [14] I have seen everything that is done under the sun, and behold, all is vanity and a striving after wind.
>
> [15] What is crooked cannot be made straight, and what is lacking cannot be counted.
>
> [16] I said in my heart, "I have acquired great wisdom, surpassing all who were over Jerusalem before me, and my heart has had great experience of wisdom and knowledge."
>
> [17] And I applied my heart to know wisdom and to know madness and folly. I perceived that this also is but a striving after wind.
>
> [18] For in much wisdom is much vexation, and he who increases knowledge increases sorrow.

Qoheleth is an analyst. He is not detached from his analysis; he is fully invested. He wants to get to the bottom of his question in 1:3, "What is the advantage in all our toil, in this vapor of life?" Qoheleth is determined to use all his available resources, which are vast. He is fully equipped with God-given wisdom (1 Kings 4:29–34). But as he surveys the task before him, he acknowledges, it is a "lousy job."[42] The job does not belong uniquely to Qoheleth, God gave it to the children of men. But Qoheleth is uniquely qualified for this "unhappy business."

Qoheleth begins with his conclusion (1:14) and says, "I have seen everything that is done under the sun, and behold, all is vapor and a striving after the wind." Everything everyone does is temporary. In the end, all our activities are trying to shepherd the wind. The reason why such an endeavor is vapor and shepherding the wind is because what is crooked cannot be straightened (1:15). We are wired to straighten crooked things, but God has only given the desire, not the necessary strength.[43] In addition to that, life under the sun is like a big puzzle, and God has made sure that some key pieces are lacking.

This reality causes Solomon to reflect on his investigation. He asserts his own qualifications (1:16). He asserts his own diligence in the lousy job (1:17a). Then he concludes that this lousy job is also trying to catch the wind. Before we think this is the end of the analysis, we need to remember that Qoheleth is taking us on a ride. He wants us to feel that frustration as well. If the wisest man looks on this unhappy business and his conclusions are that everything is mist and that the task itself is trying to catch the wind, then what chance do I have to navigate this life? Qoheleth then makes one other stark conclusion in verse 18. I paraphrase it like this: "The more you know, the more you hurt" This is Qoheleth's version of Bob Seger's famous lyric, "I wish I didn't know now what I didn't know then."[44]

---

[42] Garrett, *Proverbs, Ecclesiastes, Song of Songs*, 289.

[43] We will more fully consider the idea of straightening that which is bent at Ecclesiastes 7:13.

[44] Bob Seger, "Against the Wind," track 1 of side B on *Against the Wind*, Capitol, 1980.

If you think about life, if you wrestle with *hebel*, if you see the bent things in life, and notice some pieces are missing, you will know grief. If you take creation, life, and the fall seriously, you cannot take life lightly. This does not mean that wisdom has no advantage, it does. What it does mean is that wisdom is limited in what it can do in unlocking the mysteries of life and making sense of *hebel*. This is not Qoheleth surrendering. Instead, he moves forward knowing his limitations.

Nothing new is under the sun. Everything is merely a breath. Wisdom does not mitigate the transience of life. Laboriously laboring through the endless cycles of nature seem to intensify the brevity of life. "Do it again!" is not a reflection of wonder; it is monotony. Qoheleth, our tour guide, is not interested in relieving us of our pain yet, but be assured, this short, monotonous life is a gift. Doing laundry, changing diapers, mowing your lawn, living day after day, is a gift. There is not much new about the gift, but there is One who is making all things new, who after He has given you this short life as a gift, will give you the gift of a new creation, where the wonder of it all will never grow old. Where "do it again" will never be boring. It is in knowing Jesus, who is the One making all things new, that we gain a perspective that real profit is not found in our achievements but in His. It is in this perspective that we can enjoy the breath of life as a gift, which is a precursor to a greater one.

3

Good Gifts Make Bad Gods
(2:1–26)

Life is a vapor. What then is the advantage of a life filled with such toil? Is there anything that can mitigate the pain of *hebel*? Is there any rescue from the vapor? If Solomon can locate the profit or advantage ("that which remains"), maybe that can relieve him of the grief of a short and toilsome life. Those related questions lead Qoheleth into one of the most notorious parts of the book. We should, however, not simply read 2:1–11 as some hedonist experiment in pleasure. Instead Qoheleth is emphasizing a diligent effort for "earned pleasure." Graham Ogden notes, this is "not a self-indulgent flight, but a scientific experiment."[45]

The Pleasure Is Not Worth the Pain (2:1–11)

> [1] I said in my heart, "Come now, I will test you with pleasure; enjoy yourself." But behold, this also was vanity.
>
> [2] I said of laughter, "It is mad," and of pleasure, "What use is it?"
>
> [3] I searched with my heart how to cheer my body

---

[45] Graham Ogden, *Qoheleth*, 2nd ed. (Sheffield: Sheffield Phoenix, 2007), 43.

with wine—my heart still guiding me with wisdom—
and how to lay hold on folly, till I might see what
was good for the children of man to do under heaven
during the few days of their life.

⁴ I made great works. I built houses and planted
vineyards for myself.

⁵ I made myself gardens and parks, and planted in
them all kinds of fruit trees.

⁶ I made myself pools from which to water the forest
of growing trees.

⁷ I bought male and female slaves, and had slaves who
were born in my house. I had also great possessions
of herds and flocks, more than any who had been
before me in Jerusalem.

⁸ I also gathered for myself silver and gold and the
treasure of kings and provinces. I got singers, both
men and women, and many concubines, the delight
of the sons of man.

⁹ So I became great and surpassed all who were before
me in Jerusalem. Also my wisdom remained with me.

¹⁰ And whatever my eyes desired I did not keep from
them. I kept my heart from no pleasure, for my heart
found pleasure in all my toil, and this was my reward
for all my toil.

¹¹ Then I considered all that my hands had done and
the toil I had expended in doing it, and behold, all
was vanity and a striving after wind, and there was
nothing to be gained under the sun.

Qoheleth begins his quest by hitting the Hebrew comedy clubs
and the wine tasting rooms of Israel's finest vineyards. "I said in
my heart, 'Come now, I will test you with pleasure; enjoy yourself.'
But behold, this also was vanity" (2:1). "Pleasure" is not a negative
word. It conveys joy and gladness. "Enjoy" is literally to "look on

the good." Qoheleth is putting forth this experiment to see what profit there is in the enjoyment of life's pleasures. Will such a pursuit numb the pain of *hebel*? But before he tells us of his heroic efforts, he gives us the conclusion. "It too was *hebel*!" Pleasure is ultimately *hebel*, and so the frustration of chapter 2 is you cannot cure *hebel* with *hebel*. It fails to bring the advantage one is looking for.

Laughter and wine could not do it (2:2–3). Laughter is good for us (Ps. 126:2; Eccl. 3:4; 7:3, 6). A life without laughter is a sad life. Laughter is the spontaneous response to something that is truly funny. But laughter here is not the wholesome laughter of simple enjoyments; it's probably the idea of entertainment. Qoheleth, after summoning the best comedians in Israel found that even a good belly laugh is vapor.

Qoheleth's experiment also included some fine, clean crafted wines. This is not drunkenness, which is folly and self-destructive (Prov. 20:1; 23:29–35), but it is the use of wine as God's gift (Ps. 104:14–15). Perhaps the enjoyable use of wine could numb the pain of *hebel* and give some satisfaction to this life. Maybe there is something to self-medicating with a few good glasses of wine at the end of a rough day filled with toil and trouble. After the last glass though, the wine doesn't resolve *hebel* because it too is *hebel*.

Qoheleth says his grand experiment was to take hold of folly, that is, living a life of pleasure, to see what was "good" for the sons of Adam,[46] during the few days of their life here under heaven. In the final analysis, folly does not make *hebel* easier to live with. The diagnosis: *hebel* cannot alleviate *hebel*. So far, he's batting zero! But Qoheleth has resources, and he continues his quest by maximizing his labor, activities, and achievements (Eccl. 2:4–8).

I mentioned in the opening chapter our love of the Oregon Coast. There is a special place there called Shore Acres. It is beautiful. Hundreds of Sea Lions lay out on the rocks, sunning themselves, barking their hearts out. There is also

---

[46] The ESV says, "the children of man." The Hebrew texts says, "the sons of Adam."

a beautiful rose garden. There is a history to the rose garden,
and it is impressive. There are neatly arranged rows of roses,
each one identified by its Latin name. The garden itself is
magnificently laid out with walking paths, ponds, and gazebos.
Every time we visit, I think to myself, "Qoheleth would have
been proud." Qoheleth himself reconstructed his own private
garden of Eden. He took the dominion mandate seriously and
built houses, drew plans, acquired materials, planted vineyards,
gardens, parks, fruit trees, and developed irrigation technology.
He did it for himself, for the pure pleasure of accomplishing a
project of beauty.[47]

Furthermore, Qoheleth set out to make significant acquisitions.
He acquired solid assets (slaves and flocks) and liquid assets (gold
and silver). He obtained art and real estate. Qoheleth was on
the path of grandiose personal achievement. Not only was his
business portfolio growing, but he also sought the higher, more
cultured pleasure of music. He enjoyed the apex of art and
culture. He also obtained "concubines." The word is used only
once and is not the typical Hebrew term for concubine. Although
sexual pleasure cannot be ruled out (after all, this is Solomon),
there may be other options for the word (1 Kings 11:3).[48]

At the end of the day, Qoheleth sat upon a mountain of
wealth and achievement. His own assessment of his attainments
and position is stunning. He said, "Then I became great and
surpassed all who were before me in Jerusalem. Also, my wisdom
remained with me. And whatever my eyes desired I did not keep

---

[47] Greg Beale points out numerous aspects of King Solomon that present him as an Adam type figure who exercises dominion over the earth. See *A New Testament Biblical Theology: The Unfolding of the Old Testament in the New* (Grand Rapids: Baker Academic, 2011), 65–73.

[48] The Hebrew is uncertain. It could be "a wife and wives." The LXX renders it obscurely to as "a wine-pourer and wine-pourers." The KJV has "musical instruments," the TNK has "as well as the luxuries of commoners—coffers and coffers of them," and the NJB has "every human luxury, chest upon chest of it." See Robert D. Holmstedt, John A. Cook, and Phillip S. Marshall, *Qoheleth: A Handbook on the Hebrew Text*, ed. W. Dennis Tucker Jr., Baylor Handbook on the Hebrew Bible (Waco, TX: Baylor University Press, 2017), 93, who tentatively suggest concubines because of the context of human acquisitions.

from them. I kept my heart from no pleasure, for my heartfound pleasure in all my toil and this was my reward for all my toil" (2:9–10).

At last! Some advantage in this vaporous life was finally his. He had fame. He had unlimited resources. His accomplishments were truly epic. "I was awesome!" And yet he never lost sight of his objective as he poured himself into his work, into his pleasures, and into his plans, with wisdom. He was living the life for himself. He had a true sense of elation and satisfaction as he looked over his kingdom. But then the refrain from the Irish rock band, U2, hit him like a freight train: "But I still haven't found what I'm looking for."[49] It is as if Qoheleth said, "I took a breath after being breathless, and I realized, as I thought about all the energy and effort I poured out, it was still *hebel*. It was still trying to rope the wind. There was nothing to be gained after all. It was just an empire of dirt."[50]

"The value hard work has is the pleasure one feels in doing it (2:10), but no amount of work can produce material benefits that can be grasped and permanently gained 'under the sun' (2:11)."[51] There is nothing inherently wrong with a good laugh, a glass of wine, or personal achievement. There is nothing wrong with enjoying music or intimacy with one's spouse. But these things can never satisfy the heart in and of themselves. The very things that Qoheleth thought would vaporize *hebel* get vaporized by *hebel*. "Happiness is a vanishing vapor. All our bubbles burst eventually."[52] The bubbles we think will make us happy will indeed burst. We better be sure that we have something more substantial than bubbles.

---

[49] U2, "I Still Haven't Found What I'm Looking For," track 2 on *The Joshua Tree*, Island, 1987.

[50] "My empire of dirt" is a line from Nine Inch Nails's "Hurt," as written by Trent Reznor. See, Nine Inch Nails, "Hurt," track 14 on *The Downward Spiral*, Nothing, TVT, Interscope, 1994. The Johnny Cash video of this song powerfully portrays Qoheleth's point. You can access it here: Johnny Cash, "Hurt," https://www.youtube.com/watch?v=8AHCfZTRGiI.

[51] Farmer, *Proverbs and Ecclesiastes*, 157.

[52] Gibson, *Living Life Backwards*, 41.

Death Comes to Us All (2:12–17)

> [12] So I turned to consider wisdom and madness and folly. For what can the man do who comes after the king? Only what has already been done.
>
> [13] Then I saw that there is more gain in wisdom than in folly, as there is more gain in light than in darkness.
>
> [14] The wise person has his eyes in his head, but the fool walks in darkness. And yet I perceived that the same event happens to all of them.
>
> [15] Then I said in my heart, "What happens to the fool will happen to me also. Why then have I been so very wise?" And I said in my heart that this also is vanity.
>
> [16] For of the wise as of the fool there is no enduring remembrance, seeing that in the days to come all will have been long forgotten. How the wise dies just like the fool!
>
> [17] So I hated life, because what is done under the sun was grievous to me, for all is vanity and a striving after wind.

The investigation continues. This section (2:12–16) resumes the discussion from 1:16–18. Qoheleth is going to "face" wisdom, madness, and folly.[53] Why does Qoheleth include madness and folly? He is probably reminding us of the inclusive nature of his investigation; nothing was off the table. The bottom line is that Qoheleth is not going to kick wisdom to the curb. He will not give up on wisdom. It is the next line that challenges interpreters. "For what can the man do who comes after the king? Only what has already been done" (2:12b). The difficult sentence centers on the identity of the king. Gibson comments, "Is a human likely to come along who will be better than the king— Adam—whom God made long ago? In context this line states that there is little chance that humans will behave with greater

---

[53] The phrase, "And I turned to see" is a deliberate act of facing something to gain better perception.

wisdom than their first ancestor, Adam, who came directly from the hand of God."[54] There could be a play on words. Perhaps Qoheleth is suggesting that "nobody is going to come along and solve the mystery, neither King Adam nor King Solomon. Who can do more than he has done in exploring this mystery?"[55]

Solomon describes what he saw: "Then I saw that there is more gain in wisdom than in folly, as there is more gain in light than in darkness" (2:13). The pursuit of worldly and material success and pleasure could never bring ultimate satisfaction. Qoheleth's diagnosis: wisdom is the only way to get the advantage. He knows wisdom has its limitations, but at the end of the day, he refuses to give up on wisdom. "Limited it may be, but it is still indispensable.... As God's gift it is light; as man's possession it is sight."[56]

Wisdom is not only light, but it is also sight. The wise person, says Solomon, "has his eyes in his head," which is to say that he can see. The fool, on the other hand, "walks in darkness" (cf. Prov. 4:18–19; 22:3). As Qoheleth turns to ponder, and maybe even reassess wisdom and folly, his conclusion is crystal clear: wisdom is better than folly just as sure as light is better than darkness and sight is better than blindness. But don't think wisdom cures everything. He continues, "And yet I perceived that the same event happens to them all" (Eccl. 2:14b). Qoheleth kept looking and he saw that one "event" befalls both the wise and foolish. Although wisdom is better than folly, wisdom encounters a massive limitation: it cannot stop death. The wise man dies just like the fool. The end of *hebel* is death. Death is the sudden period at the end of the vapor. "Yes, it is better to be able to see

---

[54] Gibson, *Living Life Backwards*, 41.

[55] The comparison of Solomon to Adam is interesting and lines up with Beale's insightful observations that Solomon is a King-Adam figure. *A New Testament Biblical Theology: The Unfolding of the Old Testament in the New*, 65–73.

[56] Michael A. Eaton, *Ecclesiastes: An Introduction and Commentary*, vol. 18 of *Tyndale Old Testament Commentaries* (Downers Grove, IL: InterVarsity Press, 1983), 81.

where you are going but don't expect wisdom to save you from the fate common to all living things."[57]

This is most troubling to our tour guide. He does not like where this journey has led. Paraphrasing Qoheleth's reflections in 2:16 on the inevitable sound like this: "If I die just like the fool who couldn't care less, then why have I spent so much time being wise? As I reflected on this, it was vapor! The fool is vapor. His folly is vapor. The wise man is vapor. His wisdom is vapor. Both will die, both will be forgotten." After this sobering reflection, Qoheleth summarizes his investigation so far. The audience waits eagerly for the tour guide to explain it all as the ride slowly rolls to its first stop he says, "So I hated life, because what is done under the sun was grievous to me, for all is vapor and a striving after wind" (2:17).

There are a few observations about Solomon's startling statement. "So I hated life!" That sounds so unspiritual. It is noteworthy that "life" is plural. No, Solomon did not have nine lives. But what he hated was the totality of his life (the plural probably captures this idea of totality). Daniel Fredericks asks,

> But why are his feelings so strong? The first reason is psychological: as in all frustrations or disappointments, his expectations are momentarily unrealistic—as if any true benefit from wisdom would have an *eternal* duration or any truly *permanent* fruit. The second reason is theological: it would hardly have been a divine curse if he were passive about the Fall or loved its impact. That Qoheleth hates life, and the grueling nature of work on a cursed earth, was nothing less than the very design of God's judgment in the first place. God himself would have failed if Qoheleth's reaction to the realities of a temporary and tragic life was less than extreme hatred.[58]

---

[58] Fredericks, "Ecclesiastes," 98.
[57] Farmer, *Proverbs and Ecclesiastes,* 158.

Fredericks is right. The expression of hatred for this life is more a mark of piety than a mark of bitterness. If Qoheleth had not felt the deep pain of *hebel*, then the curse wouldn't have been a curse. Qoheleth's bubble burst, and the joy got sucked right out of his life. He looked at his toil, he looked at his wisdom, he thought he had grasped the reward, and it became hateful to him because in the end, it was simply a breath. Nothing lasts. In addition, the toil was grievous. Everything is still vapor, and all the efforts and attainments are a great vexation to the spirit because it is still an impossible task. The hunger for more, the hunger for permanence, and the hunger for significance and reward don't just linger. They consume this brief blip on the screen we call life. The hunger is never satisfied. When we think it is, it is satisfying like Chinese food is filling. We just hunger again in half an hour. Qoheleth felt the pain of *hebel* deeply.

Life's Like a Can of Peaches (2:18–23)

> [18] I hated all my toil in which I toil under the sun, seeing that I must leave it to the man who will come after me,
>
> [19] and who knows whether he will be wise or a fool? Yet he will be master of all for which I toiled and used my wisdom under the sun. This also is vanity.
>
> [20] So I turned about and gave my heart up to despair over all the toil of my labors under the sun,
>
> [21] because sometimes a person who has toiled with wisdom and knowledge and skill must leave everything to be enjoyed by someone who did not toil for it. This also is vanity and a great evil.
>
> [22] What has a man from all the toil and striving of heart with which he toils beneath the sun?
>
> [23] For all his days are full of sorrow, and his work is a vexation. Even in the night his heart does not rest. This also is vanity.

²⁴ There is nothing better for a person than that he should eat and drink and find enjoyment in his toil. This also, I saw, is from the hand of God,

²⁵ for apart from him who can eat or who can have enjoyment?

²⁶ For to the one who pleases him God has given wisdom and knowledge and joy, but to the sinner he has given the business of gathering and collecting, only to give to one who pleases God. This also is vanity and a striving after wind.

For all who missed it the first time, Qoheleth shouts it again: "I hated all my toil in which I toil under the sun" (2:18). This is the adult version of Christmas morning during my childhood. On December 1 we would make the paper Christmas chain to count down the days until Christmas, each link inscribed with the letter of our first name, so we would not fight over whose turn it was. The tree, the music, the gatherings, and the presents— Oh, the presents!—all made each day seem like a month. The anticipation grew as each link was torn off at bedtime. Then came Christmas Eve. We couldn't stand it. We would peer out the window waiting for grandpa and grandma to arrive. We stood there for hours. We knew they would be adding to the bounty under the tree. As daylight faded, our hearts beat with excitement with every pair of headlights that came up the street. The food was set, Elvis's Christmas album was playing in the background, and then the doorbell rang. The grandparents arrived with more presents!

After the evening festivities, we were off to bed. The night watches passed slowly. Who could sleep? What was under the tree? Did I get what was on *my* list, *my* covetous little list? We left the cookies and the milk with a heartwarming note for Santa. Finally, the clock struck 4:00 a.m. We walked quietly into our parent's room and gently shook their shoulders asking, "Can we open presents now?" "Go back to bed!" they growled. We watched the clock. Anticipation would build. We went back in at 5:00 a.m.

hoping for a change of heart, an act of mercy. But no. "Back to bed," they moaned. The agony of anticipation! We thought, "This Christmas will be the best ever! But it is taking forever to get here!"

Finally, a century later, at 6:00 a.m. a hopeful sign—no more snoring from dad. Mom is stirring. With unbounded energy we ran into their room, "Can we open our stockings?" They smiled, "Go ahead." With joy we bolted into the living room and tore into our stockings. LifeSaver story book, M & M's, pencils, and a pencil sharpener, and, and, and … gum. Then the organization began. Mom and Dad took their honored seats, coffee in hand. A gift distributor was announced. After a brief debate on the house floor, we were ready to begin the best day ever.

As the presents were passed out, we sat in breathless wonder, "Could this be what I have wanted my whole life, or at least since I saw the commercial for it on Saturday morning cartoons?" After all the presents were passed out, everyone took a turn. The wrapping paper was discarded after each present was opened. We could not start the next present until the proper "Thank you" was issued. The eager anticipation gave way to, "Yes! A Cookie Monster puppet! Yes! Hot Wheels with tracks! Yes! Score! Everything on the list and more! How exciting."

We played with one toy for ten minutes and another toy for five minutes. Then we looked at our massive haul and realized, "It's over." Anti-climactic to say the least. The buildup only led to a letdown. Qoheleth describes that reality from an adult perspective. Expectations are built up. Then once they come and go, disappointment sets in. The feeling of no satisfaction falls. Depression is the result. Is all the anticipation worth such a letdown? He concludes, "So I hated life."

To make matters worse, Qoheleth is also aware that everything he toiled for, everything he acquired will be left to someone who comes after him. There is the realization that his life will end, but life will continue, and he does not know what will come after him (2:12, 18; 3:22; 6:12; 7:14; 9:3; 10:14). All his attainments will go to someone. At this point Qoheleth is tormented by this great unknown. "Who knows whether he will be wise or a fool? He will have control over all that I toiled for." This too is *hebel* (2:19).

At this point, *hebel* is not just breath but the frustration that it brings. Qoheleth is in deep despair about the fruit of his labor under the sun, knowing that his legacy will be left to one who did not earn it, will not appreciate it, and may even mismanage it. He is at his breaking point as he has tried to answer his question from 1:3: "What does man gain by all the toil at which he toils under the sun?"

After all his dubious investigation, his task has been grievous and painful. Even at night his mind does not rest because it cannot rest. Even after a day of exhausting toil, when his body, heart, and mind should be ready for rest, he cannot. He is thinking about tomorrow's toil and even what will come after he is gone. This too is *hebel*. All the grief, all the labor, all the sleepless nights, and then it is all gone.

But there is hope in his last statement of verse 23. He says, "For all his days are full of sorrow, and his work is a vexation. Even in the night his heart does not rest. This also is vanity." Yes, there is hope and it is this: "Qohelet's despair is also *hebel*. It does not endure forever. Qohelet's disappointment turns to acceptance when he learns to appreciate the ability God gives us to find enjoyment in our work."[59] In other words, the disappointment is a breath and in grasping that reality, he is empowered to see the joy of a fleeting life and all it entails.

Qoheleth is ready to give us some relief by putting together a corner of the puzzle. He is prepared to answer his question from 1:3: "What does man gain by all the toil at which he toils under the sun?" His initial, visceral conclusion of 2:11, 17, 18 ("And so I hated life") is revised. Wisdom has shed its light and brought him to a more solid perspective. As the first leg of the ride comes to an end, Qoheleth tells us, "There is nothing better for a person than that he should eat and drink and find enjoyment in his toil. This also, I saw, is from the hand of God,

---

[59] Farmer, *Proverbs and Ecclesiastes*, 158–59.

for apart from him who can eat or who can have enjoyment? For to the one who pleases him God has given wisdom and knowledge and joy, but to the sinner he has given the business of gathering and collecting, only to give to one who pleases God. This also is vanity and a striving after wind" (2:24–26).

This is far more spiritual than it sounds. "There is nothing better" is literally "This is good" and refers to that which is truly good, spiritually good in the sight of God. The conclusion is powerful: it is good for man to enjoy the simple pleasures of life, eating, drinking, and laboring under the sun. He should recognize that those simple pleasures are from the hand of God; they are indeed gifts from Him. "What spoils them is our hunger to get out of them more than what they can give."[60]

"For apart from him who can eat or who can have enjoyment" (2:25). If we live life, eating, drinking, and working, without recognizing that these are God's gifts to us; if we live life and think these things are rewards to be earned rather than gifts to be enjoyed, then *hebel* will crush us with disappointment. "For to the one who pleases him God has given wisdom and knowledge and joy" (2:26). The one who has received God's favor, God gives the gift of not only wisdom and knowledge but also enjoyment. The capacity to enjoy the gifts of God is a gift from God, "but to the sinner he has given the business of gathering and collecting, only to give to one who pleases God" (2:26). Doug Wilson makes a key observation: "The message here is twofold. God is the One who gives things, and God is the One who gives the power to enjoy things. These are distinct gifts ... just as a can of peaches and a can opener are distinct gifts. Only the first is given to the unbeliever. The believer is given both, which is simply another way of saying that he is given the capacity for enjoyment."[61]

This is the first corner of the puzzle. It is a powerful remedy for the despair caused by *hebel*. Life is a gift from God.

---

[60] Derek Kidner, *The Message of Ecclesiastes: The Bible Speaks Today* (Downers Grove, IL: InterVarsity Press, 1976), 35.

[61] Douglas Wilson, *Joy at the End of the Tether: The Inscrutable Wisdom of Ecclesiastes* (Moscow, ID: Canon Press, 1999), 17.

Labor is a gift from God. Food and drink are gifts from God. Each gift is given to us to enjoy. Life is brief. It is a passing shadow; it is a fleeting moment. But it is a gift. The last line of the corner piece, "This also is vanity and a striving after wind" (2:26), reminds us that the enjoyment of these gifts is also a breath.

However, the reality of briefly enjoying these gifts is not designed to bring another disappointment. It is designed to launch us into the relentless, vigorous pursuit of God in the enjoyment of these vaporous gifts. Don't waste your breath! Barry Webb brings these first two chapters into focus: "The possibility of enjoyment returns, significantly, only when the quest for profit is given up altogether (2:22–23) and replaced by the notion of gift. Opportunities to eat, drink, and find satisfaction in one's work, when they come, are not human achievements but divine gifts, and are to be enjoyed as such. They are only palliatives, to be sure, for they too are *hebel*, and will slip from our grip like everything else—but that is no reason to reject them."[62]

We have learned great truths! Take a breath, take it in, but don't linger too long. Qoheleth has more to teach us and is about to take us on the next ride.

---

[62] Webb, *Five Festal Garments*, 93–94.

4

Beautiful, in Its Time
(3:1–15)

We were visiting family and a relative was talking to another about a personal tragedy, and the one said to the other, "God let this happen for a reason. He has a purpose in it." What piqued my attention was that this relative was not a Bible-reader or a churchgoer, and did not profess to be born-again. This, of course, is not the first time I have heard someone say, "I know this happened for a reason." However, we must wonder, as human beings living under the sun, where do we get that innate sense that the things of life happen for a reason? The answer is found in Ecclesiastes 3. This passage will not only expound the truth of God's sovereignty over the times and events of life, but it also sets up for us an excruciating analysis of real-life challenges to enjoying the gift of a fleeting life.

Turn! Turn! Turn! (3:1–8)

¹ For everything there is a season, and a time for every matter under heaven:

² a time to be born, and a time to die;
a time to plant, and a time to pluck up what is planted;

³ a time to kill, and a time to heal;
a time to break down, and a time to build up;

⁴ a time to weep, and a time to laugh;
a time to mourn, and a time to dance;

⁵ a time to cast away stones, and a time to gather stones together;
a time to embrace, and a time to refrain from embracing;

⁶ a time to seek, and a time to lose;
a time to keep, and a time to cast away;

⁷ a time to tear, and a time to sew;
a time to keep silence, and a time to speak;

⁸ a time to love, and a time to hate;
a time for war, and a time for peace.

This passage has served as a chart topper at least twice. The first was for the Byrds in 1965 with "Turn, Turn, Turn." The second was for Ray Stevens in 1970 with "Everything is Beautiful." This poem on time in 3:1–8 is probably the most famous part of Ecclesiastes. But its function in the book serves a larger and more profound purpose than radio play. Qoheleth has laid out his first conclusion in chapter two. Success, wisdom, achievement, pleasure, and even wisdom cannot change the fact that life is a vapor. None of those pursuits provide the advantage that Qoheleth was looking for. Trying to mitigate *hebel* with *hebel* is a bust.

The first glorious discovery is that although life is a vapor, it is a gift, and the gift is to be enjoyed. Perhaps Qoheleth could have ended the book there, but if he did, he would not be a faithful guide to the end of the journey. He will not let us off the hook so easily. He is not going to stop exploring his nagging question from 1:3: "What is the advantage in our toil?" He still has more to teach us, and he begins the next lesson with a beautiful poem that is designed to bring about some more hard turns, bumps, and jolts. Maybe even a bruise or two.

The opening line is an unwavering declaration. The NASB is more straightforward than the ESV here. It reads, "There is an appointed time for everything. And there is a time for every event under heaven." This truth will be echoed in 3:11 and 3:17. Who sets the time for everything? Who plans for every event under heaven? It is God who does this (3:11). The poem that follows is composed of twenty-eight items, fourteen couplets, both of which are multiples of seven. The numeric structure underscores that Qoheleth is poetically stressing the completeness and totality of life. The couplets themselves capture both the universality and comprehensiveness of God's control. They form merisms, that is bookends of events that entail everything in between.[63] The couplets encapsulate completeness or wholeness.

The poem itself must be understood, not as something we are supposed to do, but rather as what God does. Gibson puts it this way, "We are each writing the story of our lives, but we are not the main author."[64] God has appointed these events and every event in between. This is a deeply profound statement of God's absolute sovereignty. He is "working out all things after the counsel of his will" (Eph. 1:11). Truly, "from him, and through him, and unto him are all things" (Rom. 11:36). He is the God who ordains the times and events in our lives.

Qoheleth proceeds to then unfold this truth through the remaining couplets. The first couplet emphasizes the totality of life (Eccl. 3:2). From the cradle to the grave, from life's first cry, to the final breath, God appoints the day of one's birth and the day of one's death, and every day between (Job 14:5; Ps. 139:16). Truly, our times are in His hands (Ps. 31:15).

The second couplet deals with sowing and reaping (Eccl. 3:2). The point is that hard work, from beginning to end, is in the hand of God's providence. It is not just the harvest, which is in the hand of God, it is hard work of sowing as well. The third and fourth couplets (3:3) encompass, on the one hand, the events of war, capital punishment, or self-defense, and, on the other

---

[63] Merisms are used frequently in Scripture, where two parts, often opposing parts, are used to designate the whole. "Day and night," "rising up and sitting down," "heaven and earth," "head and foot," are common examples.

[64] Gibson, *Living Life Backwards*, 52.

hand, seeking to repair and heal what has been ruined. Both the destructive and constructive are under God's sovereignty.

The fifth couplet is weeping and laughing while the sixth couplet is mourning and dancing (3:4). Both couplets reflect the emotional ups and downs of life that are outside our control. Our lives are not sitcom TV sets where we get the "laugh now" prompt. We don't schedule times to cry. Those times just happen.

The seventh couplet is throwing and gathering stones while the eighth couplet is embracing and shunning (3:5). These two couplets have puzzled commentators. "Stones" seem intentionally vague. Stones could be used for building materials or weapons. The rabbis took the first line to refer to marital intimacy, engaging and abstaining from sexual relations. The next line seems to affirm there are times when embracing is appropriate and other times when it is inappropriate.

The ninth and tenth couplets deal with stuff that gets lost, stuff that gets accumulated, and the stuff that gets hoarded by pack rats (3:6). Garrett sums up the ninth and tenth couplets, "Nothing in this world is ours forever."[65] The eleventh (tear apart/ sew together) and twelfth (silent/speak) couplets fit well together (3:7). "Tear apart" may be a reference to mourning while "sew" may refer to repairing the garment of grief. The time to be silent and the time to speak has echoes of Job's three friends. When to speak and when to stay silent is a matter of wisdom.[66]

The final two couplets are "a time to love" and "a time to hate" and also "a time for war" and "a time for peace" (3:8). These couplets correspond since they speak of human relationships on both the personal and national level.

The precise nature of every one of these couplets could be debated indefinitely. However, the point is clear that all the events that take place under the sun are determined by God. Every birth, every death, every word, every deed, whether constructive

---

[65] Garrett, *Proverbs, Ecclesiastes, Song of Songs*, 298.
[66] See Proverbs 10:19; 11:12; 17:28.

or destructive, whether good or evil, happy or sad, comes from a divine appointment. Qoheleth holds fast to the sovereignty of God. He will revisit it in coming chapters, however, Qoheleth uses this beautiful poem not to comfort us, but to press us hard with another question.

Eternity in the Heart (3:9–11)

The nagging question of 1:3 is repeated in 3:9: "What gain has the worker from his toil?" In light of God's comprehensive sovereignty, Qoheleth returns to the question of advantage. Perhaps the knowledge of God's purposes will bring some advantage to the toil with which we toil. If we could see *how* the pieces fit together, *why* the pieces fit together, then maybe we could gain some solace in the mist, some perspective in the fog.

Qoheleth tells us that he observed the "business" or the "task" that God has given to the children of men to keep them busy. But what is the task? Walt Kaiser sums it up, "God has also implanted in the hearts of men a desire to know how his plan makes all the details fit together.... This quest is a deep-seated desire, compulsive drive, because people are made in the image of God and are made to appreciate the beauty of creation (on an aesthetic level); to know the character, composition, and meaning of the world (on an academic and philosophical level); and to discern its purpose and destiny (on a theological level)."[67] In other words, we are wired to want to understand God's plan.

Here is what we know: "God has made everything beautiful in His time" (3:11a, *author's translation* and KJV). Some translations say, "He has made all things appropriate in its time."[68] The NET Bible captures both elements of the verse and says, "Everything fit beautifully in its appropriate time." We know the times and events of life happen for a reason, the reason is

---

[67] Kaiser, *Coping with Change: Ecclesiastes* (Ross-Shire, Scotland: Christian Focus, 2013), 101.

[68] Two translations adopting the word "appropriate" are the CSB and the NASB. Three that instead use the word "beautiful" are the ESV, the KJV, and the NIV.

a good one, and it is a part of God's beautiful plan. God is the cosmic artist, and we are made in His image. Therefore, we have an innate sense of reason and purpose in the events of life.

Furthermore, God has put eternity in our hearts (3:11b). We not only have an inherent knowledge that God has a plan, but we have an inherent sense of eternity and the Eternal One. Consequently, the details of life matter to us. The events of life are not random, but they have a specific design that fits into an eternal plan. We have an innate sense that it is our task to figure out the reasons, put the pieces together, and see the big picture.

However, even in this there is a big letdown, at least for now. God has not given us the capacity to figure everything out and understand the reason why things happen the way they do. God has not allowed us to look upon the canvas and see the full picture of what is being painted. This leads to profound frustration. Gibson says, "If we could see the end from the beginning and understand how a billion lives and a thousand generations and unspeakable sorrows and untold joys are all woven into a tapestry of perfect beauty then we would be God."[69]

The Good Portion (3:12–14)

The question of verse 9 and the observations of verses 10–11 combine to make us feel the frustration of our God-imposed limitations. As finite people we are profoundly restricted in our understanding of this life. Our frustration stems from the earnest desire to want to know the plan and how the details fit together in the tapestry. But we do not and cannot. Think of the comfort we would feel if we only knew *why*. Think of the frustration when we find out that the God who wired us to want to know why has also denied us the ability and insight. Belief in the sovereignty of God is vital to faith in God, but it never gives us some kind of special sight or understanding into the events of life.

---

[69] Gibson, *Living Life Backwards*, 59.

Do we see what Solomon has done? He has expounded the comprehensive sovereignty of God over the times and events of life. He has told us what we already know. He told us that God has put us together so that we know there is a reason for everything and that God has a plan that really does fit together. And then God has said that even though I made you to want to know, I will not let you peer into my secret council.

We seem to be left hanging. God wired us to want to know and then will not let us know! What frustration! But in verse 12, Qoheleth then gives us another statement about what he knows (ESV, "perceived") so we are not left in despair. What does he know? He repeats the key text from 2:24–26 that there is "nothing better for us than to rejoice and do good in one's lifetime." Rejoice! Be glad you know the sovereign God! Be thankful for your life; it's a gift. Devote yourself to doing good, living a life of faithfulness (3:12–13). There is no fatalism here, but more pieces of the puzzle are added to that corner. Qoheleth's counsel to us is abandon all hope of full comprehension of God's plan, be glad, and do good. "The answer to an unhealthy preoccupation with finding the answers and reasons for all of one's troubles is to enjoy what you have to enjoy, including your toil, without trying to figure out some sort of ultimate leverage of advantage from it."[70]

What We Know and What God Seeks (3:14–15)

Before we leave this section, one more observation about our sovereign God (3:14–15). What God does is forever. His work is not *hebel*. What God does is perfect, you cannot add or take away from it. God has worked so that we would fear Him. The perplexity of wanting to understand the work of God and then being unable to understand it serves a purpose. "This frustration is deliberately imposed by God so that human beings will always be able to recognize the difference between themselves

---

[70] Jeffrey Meyers, *A Table in the Mist: Ecclesiastes Through New Eyes* (Monroe, LA: Athanasius, 2006), 70.

and their Maker and defer to him."[71] It is enough to know that
God is sovereign, wise, and working out His plan. It is enough
to know He is making all things beautiful in His time. If we
know this, then we know our biggest responsibility, or *summum
bonum*, is not to be some sleuth trying to solve the mystery,
but to be one who fears and trusts the God who is making all
things beautiful.

Verse 15 is elusive. "That which is, already has been; that
which is to be, already has been; and God seeks what has been
driven away." The NIV translates the last line, "God will call
the past to account."[72] The verse serves as a transition to the
following sections which will deal with injustice and oppression.

It may be that Qoheleth is asserting in light of God's sovereignty
that what has been done is done. What is going to be done will be
just like that which has gone before. The events he is alluding to
are probably the bad things of this life. But even though God is
sovereign over the bad things, He will call everything to account,
even the past stuff, seemingly long forgotten. Perhaps the point is
that God remembers and seeks out both the past which has been
forgotten and those who have been forgotten, assuring them that
they are not forgotten. "It is all the events of human history that
time has chased away into the past, and to us these are gone and
lost forever. But not to God. He will dial back time and fetch the
past into his present to bring it to account."[73]

Conclusion

What we have considered in this chapter is significant to the
overall message of Ecclesiastes. God calls us to trust Him and
fear Him as our sovereign God, who is over all the details of
our lives. As we ache to know the reason for the painful events
of our lives, God tells us that He knows that we want to know,

---

[71] Webb, *Five Festal Garments*, 94.
[72] Instead of the NIV's "God will call the past to account," the Tanakh (Jewish Pub-
lications Society) reads, "God seeks the pursued." Garrett makes a compelling case for
this latter translation. See Garrett, *Proverbs, Ecclesiastes, Song of Songs*, 300–2.
[73] Gibson, *Living Life Backwards*, 58.

but He won't let us. Instead of being a great cryptanalyst, deciphering the work of God, He calls us to enjoy this short life, live for Him, trust Him, keep the right perspective on life, and know He will not forget any of the things of the past. All things will be made right. God is making all things beautiful in His time. How can we be sure? Because in the fullness of time, God sent forth His Son (Gal. 4:4–7). Because at the right time, Christ died for the ungodly (Rom. 5:6). Because when God called each of us, He called us at the acceptable time (2 Cor. 6:2). Because God exalts the humble at the proper time (1 Pet. 5:6). If you are suffering, be confident since God is the cosmic artist, making everything beautiful. Trust Him as the One who has written you into His story. Trust Him as the One who is over the details of your life. Trust Him because He has already given His Son for you. Lean on Him.

On April 27, 2016, I had a large brain tumor removed in an 11-and-a-half-hour surgery. For my first sermon back in the pulpit, I had planned to preach Psalm 131. In God's providence, I would not give that sermon from my pulpit but rather from a hospital bed. I went back in for a wound revision. Then, the morning we were going to leave after the follow-up surgery, I had a cardiac episode and ended up back in the hospital. The doctors discovered a hematoma in my brain. The cardiac episode was a mystery. I went through tests, blood patches for potential spinal leaks, and the list could go on.

That Sunday morning, I was not at Grace Community Church in Minden, Nevada. I was in a hospital bed at the University of California San Francisco, Parnassus campus. My wife, my sister, and my niece were with me. I asked for my Bible, and I told them, "This was the text I was going to preach this morning at church, but it is still just as relevant in this hospital bed: 'O LORD, my heart is not lifted up; my eyes are not raised too high; I do not occupy myself with things too great and too marvelous for me. But I have calmed and quieted my soul, like a weaned child with its mother; like a weaned child is my soul within me. O Israel, hope in the LORD from this time forth and forevermore'" (Ps. 131:1–3).

We want to know the things that are "too great and too marvelous" for us. But humility drives us to say, "I will not occupy myself with those things. They are far above my pay grade!" Humility also says, "It is not that I will abandon my pursuit to know those things, but it is a matter of calming and quieting my soul." The child who has not been weaned is only content when at his mother's breast, otherwise the child is restless and fretting. The weaned child is content to simply rest in his mother's arms.[74] He no longer needs to be nursing to be content. This is a picture of believers who no longer need the infant comforts from their Father but have learned to be content in their strong God who takes care of them. Our hope is not in unraveling the mystery, but in hoping in God, both now and forever.

---

[74] The imagery in Ps. 131:1–3 is strikingly beautiful as God is portrayed as a mother who has both nursed and weaned her child.

5

The Gathering Storm Clouds
(3:16–4:16)

When we come to embrace God's sovereignty over our lives and the world; when we come to believe that every event is under His sovereign wisdom; when we come to believe that our calling is to enjoy this life as a gift and trust God in the mysteries, then we are immediately confronted by a multitude of issues that bring into question the beauty of God's plan and make it difficult to enjoy life as a gift. In this section we are going to outline a series of challenges and confront them.

Challenge One: Injustice (3:16–22)

> [16] Moreover, I saw under the sun that in the place of justice, even there was wickedness, and in the place of righteousness, even there was wickedness.
>
> [17] I said in my heart, God will judge the righteous and the wicked, for there is a time for every matter and for every work.
>
> [18] I said in my heart with regard to the children of man that God is testing them that they may see that they themselves are but beasts.
>
> [19] For what happens to the children of man and what happens to the beasts is the same; as one dies, so dies

the other. They all have the same breath, and man has no advantage over the beasts, for all is vanity.

[20] All go to one place. All are from the dust, and to dust all return.

[21] Who knows whether the spirit of man goes upward and the spirit of the beast goes down into the earth?

[22] So I saw that there is nothing better than that a man should rejoice in his work, for that is his lot. Who can bring him to see what will be after him?

Injustice is not the way it is supposed to be. Justice and righteousness are the way things ought to be. Wickedness shoves justice out of the way and replaces righteousness. Injustice and evil vandalize shalom. People are willing to abuse a widow or orphan for a buck. Some are willing to take advantage of the elderly for a loaf of bread. Others will take a bribe to pervert justice, allowing pride and greed to govern in the place of principle and virtue. Man lives by the law of the jungle. Lawlessness is his law.

The righteous man asks, "Will justice ever prevail?" Does not the presence of injustice and wickedness ruin God's plan to make everything beautiful? Does it not threaten my ability to enjoy the gift? In response, Qoheleth quickly reminds us that there will be payday someday (Eccl. 3:17).[75] In Qoheleth's world, the pervasive view was that actions were punished or rewarded under the sun. Qoheleth's realism is not so naïve. People don't always get what they deserve now. But they will, one day. God will judge both the righteous and the wicked. It is a part of His plan. In that sense, it is even a part of His plan to make everything beautiful in His time.

Qoheleth reminds us of another fact: man, the beast, is a vapor (3:18–20). God tests man to show him that he is a beast. After the fall human beings became beasts, closer to animals than to God.

---

[75] The phrase "pay day someday" was popularized by a famous sermon preached by R. G. Lee, "Pay-Day Someday." He preached it over 1,200 times in various settings. One can access the sermon here: https://www.youtube.com/watch?v=HHd-SP53f3IQ.

"God proves to humanity through the recurring curse of death that we are animals, finite mammals who are also merely God's creations: equally subject to his will; equally dust; equally distant from his infinite transcendence."[76] God is showing man that the wise, the fool, and the stupid alike perish, just like the beasts. "Their graves are their homes forever, their dwelling places to all generations, though they called lands by their own names. Man in his pomp will not remain; he is like the beasts that perish" (Ps. 49:11–12).

Man and beast have the same breath, that is, the same animating life principle. They both go to the same place, that is, the grave, the ground, the dust. The man who lives like a dog will die like one too. No benefit. All is breath. "From the sole perspective of breathing and dying, since the Fall, humans truly do not have an advantage over animals."[77] "Dust and breath are not a stable combination."[78] As long as man perverts justice and abandons righteousness, he is like an animal, not an image-bearer.

In Ecclesiastes 3:21, Qoheleth states, "Who knows whether the spirit of man goes upward, and the spirit of the beast goes down into the earth?" His words have the ring of agnosticism about the afterlife to it. However, Qoheleth is affirming that although man may act like a beast, he is more than a beast. He is not stating some agnostic sentiment about the afterlife, but rather he is expressing the nearly universal ignorance and neglect of the afterlife among the sons of men. He is questioning whether man knows anything about that reality or even thinks about it. As Duane Garret notes, "Ecclesiastes does not deny afterlife but does force the reader to take death seriously."[79]

Qoheleth repeats the refrain in verse 22 and says, "I have seen that nothing is better than that man should be happy in his activities, for that is his lot. For who will bring him to see what

---

[76] Fredericks, "Ecclesiastes," 121.
[77] Fredericks, "Ecclesiastes," 122.
[78] Fredericks, "Ecclesiastes," 122.
[79] Garrett, *Proverbs, Ecclesiastes, Song of Songs,* 305.

will occur after him?" This is Qoheleth's tactic to prevent us from being too comfortable. Rejoice in your work but know you will die, and you don't know what will happen to all your stuff. But what can you do about it? Some may think that Qoheleth would win more converts if he didn't bring up death so often, but that is his whole point. We all die. We are all a breath. The unjust and the wicked are a breath. God will judge them.

Injustice and death do not bring God's beauty into disrepute or derail our joy. Injustice should anger us. Wickedness should make us indignant. Neither is the way things ought to be. We should do what we can to fight against it. But man is a brute beast after the fall and man like the brute beast will die, and when he does, God will be waiting with perfect justice, in His time. God's justice is part of Him making all things beautiful in His time. In the meantime, don't lose sight of the gift.

Challenge Two: Oppression (4:1–3)

> ¹ Again I saw all the oppressions that are done under the sun. And behold, the tears of the oppressed, and they had no one to comfort them! On the side of their oppressors there was power, and there was no one to comfort them.
>
> ² And I thought the dead who are already dead more fortunate than the living who are still alive.
>
> ³ But better than both is he who has not yet been and has not seen the evil deeds that are done under the sun.

Oppression, the evil sibling of injustice, now appears to threaten the beauty of God's plan and our enjoyment. Qoheleth is not some aristocrat who was detached from the pain of humanity. Rather he saw the acts of oppression and saw the tears of the oppressed. He agonized that there was no one to comfort them and that the oppressors had all the power. For emphasis, he repeats, "There was no one to comfort them." The oppressed do not have the opportunity to simply enjoy their labor as the gift of God because they are taken advantage of and beaten down. The most basic of God's gifts are violently torn from them and nobody does anything about it.

Qoheleth comes to a dark conclusion in verses 2–3. From the perspective of the oppressed, death or even non-existence seems to be a better alternative. As Timothy Keller reminds us,

> Only a small number of people in the history of the world have lived in relatively "safe" conditions. War, injustice, oppression, famine, natural disaster, family breakdown, disease, mental illness, physical disability, racism, crime, scarcity of resources, class struggle—these 'social problems' are the results of our alienation from God. They bring deep misery and violence to the lives of most humanity. The majority of people who read this book, however, probably belong to the relatively small group of folk who, through God's kindness, lead an existence generally free from these forces. This comparative comfort can isolate us in a fictious world where suffering is difficult to find. But this isolation is fragile, for suffering surrounds us—even in the suburbs![80]

Our hearts should ache over the injustice and oppression that exists in this death row cell under the sun. These things seem to pose a real challenge to joy and beauty.

Challenge Three: Envy (4:4–6)

> [4] Then I saw that all toil and all skill in work come from a man's envy of his neighbor. This also is vanity and a striving after wind.

> [5] The fool folds his hands and eats his own flesh.

---

[80] Timothy Keller, *Ministries of Mercy* (Philipsburg: P & R, 1997), 13.

⁶ Better is a handful of quietness than two hands full
of toil and a striving after wind.

Qoheleth moves from the cruelty that exists because of oppression to the misery caused by idolatrous competition. Labor is a gift, but it becomes an idol if it is fueled by envy. The man Qoheleth has in view is skilled and works hard, but he works hard just to get on top. He is simply driven to be better and have more than his neighbor. This man sees what Jones has, wants it, and wants more. This is more than merely "keeping up with the Jones." This is a matter of trying to leave the Joneses in the dust, choking on their fumes. But it is a vapor and trying to shepherd the wind. After all, how long can someone stay on top? How much enjoyment can one have making sure that all one's competitors are beaten back down the hill of success? What is the point of being on the top bunk in a death row cell anyway?

Some might say, "You are right! No reason getting devoured in a dog-eat-dog world. I am not going to be greedy; I am going to relax and play video games!" Qoheleth says that is the response of a fool. Idleness is not the answer because it is folly and self-destructive. As we learn in Proverbs, "A little sleep, a little slumber, a little folding of the hands to rest and poverty will come upon you like a robber and want like an armed man" (Prov. 6:10–11). Michael Eaton says that the condition of the lazy is "analyzed as self-cannibalism."[81]

Excessive toil may be foolish and counterproductive, but we are fools if we fold our hands, wait for a government check, and starve to death. Qoheleth reminds us that neither the sluggard nor the envy-driven workaholic is a model for anyone. The way of wisdom is found in Ecclesiastes 4:6. Do not be consumed with envy and rivalry and work your life away because you want to be richer and better than your neighbor. But don't sit at home and play Candy Crush all day either, boasting how non-materialistic you are. The way to really live this life which God has given you is to balance your toil with rest. Take a day off.

---

[81] Eaton, *Ecclesiastes*, 93.

Remember the Sabbath. Rest and relaxation are vital for enjoying the gift of life which is filled with so much labor.

I wish I would have had this perspective when I was in seminary. I worked hard in seminary—really, really hard. Academic excellence and achievement became my idol. My wife asked many times if I could take a Saturday off from studying and take her and our daughter to the park for a picnic, but I was far too determined to ace the next exam. My commitment to *hebel* and striving after the wind made our marriage a miserable one. Thanks be to God, He brought me to repentance and restored us. Qoheleth's advice would have been, "Listen, it is O.K. to get a B on your next Hebrew exam if it means spending much needed time with your wife. That grade, ten years from now will not matter. By the way, no one will ask you what your GPA was. Get some rest, enjoy your family, and take the B."

Challenge Four: Loneliness (4:7–12)

⁷ Again, I saw vanity under the sun:

⁸ one person who has no other, either son or brother, yet there is no end to all his toil, and his eyes are never satisfied with riches, so that he never asks, "For whom am I toiling and depriving myself of pleasure?" This also is vanity and an unhappy business.

The next portrait in Qoheleth's gallery of "challenges to enjoying the gift" is the guy who is married to his work (4:7–8). Qoheleth says he sees another vapor under the sun and that is the person who has no dependents. Perhaps this man has no spouse, certainly no son or brother. He is alone. And yet he works himself to death. There is no end to his toil. He is never satisfied with money, and he has never asked the right question, "For whom am I toiling and depriving myself of pleasure?" How much misery could be averted if only we asked ourselves the right question? Even though there was no one with whom to share his life, this lonely person devoted himself to endless labor.

A lonely life is a sad life, no matter how much money a person has. Derek Thomas reports, "John Paul Getty,[82] before his death, said, 'I've never known love or what it means to have a friend.'"[83] Doug Wilson observes, "A man works hard to make a pile and doesn't stop to ask a very basic question—why am I doing this? He can't afford to marry or have children, because they would take him away from his work. He cannot afford to have friends because all their motives would be suspect. He could buy dinner for everyone in the restaurant, but no one wants to sit with him. That's all right, because he doesn't want to sit with them either."[84] In the end, marriage to one's work is a miserable marriage, and toil makes a lousy spouse.

The Blessing of Companionship (4:9–12)

Companionship is also the gift of God, and it makes life and labor sweeter. Unless the benefits of hard work are shared with someone you love, toil has no gain. When kept within the perspectives of *hebel*, blessings shared become blessings doubled.

> [9] Two are better than one, because they have a good reward for their toil.
>
> [10] For if they fall, one will lift up his fellow. But woe to him who is alone when he falls and has not another to lift him up!
>
> [11] Again, if two lie together, they keep warm, but how can one keep warm alone?
>
> [12] And though a man might prevail against one who is alone, two will withstand him—a threefold cord is not quickly broken.

This famous passage, appropriately read at weddings, is a picture of the comfort and strength of companionship in a

---

[82] John Paul Getty was at one time the wealthiest man in America.

[83] Derek Thomas, "Ecclesiastes 4: The Quandary of Oppression," (sermon given at First Presbyterian Church, Jackson, MS, 6 July 2003). Access the text of the sermon here: https://fpcjackson.org/resource-library/sermons/an-empty-life-6-the-quandary-of-oppression/.

[84] Wilson, *Joy at the End of the Tether*, 61.

harsh world. There is safety in companionship. There is better profit in companionship. There is warmth in companionship. A third cord is even better. The third cord is often thought to be another person, even the Lord Himself. It is noteworthy that Qoheleth does not label companionship as *hebel*.[85] Friendship is invaluable. It is the antidote to the lonely life of the workaholic. Hugh Black summarizes the blessings of friendship, "To have a heart that we can trust, and into which we can pour our griefs, our doubts, and our fears, is already to take the edge from the grief, and the sting from doubt, and the shade from fear.... Joy also demands that its joy should be shared.... A simple generous friendship will thus add to the joy and will divide the sorrow."[86]

Challenge Five: Politics (4:13–16)

The final challenge to enjoying the gift and to God making all things beautiful is politics. Some might think if we could get the right king, the right president, the right congress, the right parliament, then all would be well. But politics are a vapor too. With the vaporous nature of politics comes frustration with politics.

> [13] Better was a poor and wise youth than an old and foolish king who no longer knew how to take advice.
>
> [14] For he went from prison to the throne, though in his own kingdom he had been born poor.
>
> [15] I saw all the living who move about under the sun, along with that youth who was to stand in the king's place.
>
> [16] There was no end of all the people, all of whom he led. Yet those who come later will not rejoice in him. Surely this also is vanity and a striving after wind.

---

[85] Farmer astutely recognizes the value of friendship with these words: "Working to achieve community seems to promise more lasting rewards than simply working to become rich." See, Farmer, *Proverbs and Ecclesiastes*, 165.

[86] Hugh Black, *The Art of Being a Good Friend* (Manchester, NH: Heritage, 2019), 38–39.

Qoheleth, who knew politics, admits that one kind of politician is better than another. The poor man comes from the people and knows the plight of the people. He is a common man, but he is also a wise man. The old foolish king doesn't listen to anybody, won't receive counsel, and assumes the "riff raff" doesn't know anything. The poor wise man is a real success story. He went from a prison cell to the throne. It could be that he had been a political prisoner or in debtor's prison. He has humble origins but ascends to the throne. His approval ratings are through the roof. Everybody loves this guy. The phrase "no end to all the people, to all who were before them" could refer to the king's popularity. But the reality is that "today's hero is tomorrow's bum."[87] The sentiment that "happy days are here again" is a vapor. The reign of a good king is as temporary as a breath.

It is true that some rulers are better than others. We should want good, wise, righteous leaders. We should resist tyrants. But presidents come and presidents go. The "great hope" for the next election will have his disaffected followers in time. They will want a fresh face. Kidner notes, "He (the young king) too will go the way of the old king, not necessarily for his faults, but simply as time and familiarity, and the restlessness of men, make him no longer interesting."[88] Politics brings no lasting change. Oftentimes it is nothing more than a debacle of the fickle. It challenges our joy if our joy is in human kings. It appears to challenge God's beauty if we are expecting any son of Adam other than Jesus Christ to bring hope and change.

We need to guard our hearts against these realities that threaten the enjoyment of the gift of this short life. They may be dark hues in His masterpiece, but the truth is that none of these challenges put a dent in God's beautiful plan. We should not ignore oppression or injustice. We should not tolerate envy, greed, or isolation. We should not be consumed in politics as if it were our only hope or only interest. Instead, we should receive rest and companionship as gifts from God's gracious hand.

---

[87] Kaiser, *Coping with Change*, 113.
[88] Kidner, *The Message of Ecclesiastes*, 52.

With grateful hearts, we should look to Him alone. As David said, "Some trust in chariots and some in horses, but we trust in the name of the LORD our God" (Ps. 20:7).

6

Watch Your Step
(5:1–7)

Qoheleth is going to resume the challenges to our enjoyment in Ecclesiastes 5:8–6:12. But before he continues the tour through the gallery of sadness, he will take what appears to be a detour. He has taken us through the depressing portraits of injustice and oppression. He has vividly captured the self-inflicted miseries of this life through our labor and the joy-killing rivalry with others. He has shined a spotlight on our toil and joy-killing isolation. He has painted the relevant picture of the fickle relationship with political leaders, where loyalties shift with the wind and leaders disappoint. Now he will address, with intense seriousness, our relationship with God. But since he resumes addressing challenges to our enjoyment in 5:8, we are left wondering, "What is the connection between 3:16–4:16 and 5:1–7?"

The lesson so far has been if we are going to enjoy this short life, we must see all its various elements and aspects as the gifts of God. Joy in living comes from a God-centered, God-ordered life. Qoheleth tackled those parts of life that threaten to deplete our joy. He then relentlessly pointed us to God. His audience, ancient and contemporary, may conclude that what we really need then, to round out our lives, is some religion.

After all, if we can't enjoy life without God, maybe we need a little more God in our lives. This is dangerous logic because God is not to be trifled with. Yes, life revolves around Him, and our response to Him in worship is vital in our short lives. But worship is also dangerous because we are dealing with God. The God to whom we must give account, is not the cosmic grandpa, nor the divine Santa Claus. He is God, the Lord of heaven and earth. Qoheleth would have probably nodded in agreement with Gordon Dahl's famous statement: "We worship our work, work at our play, and play at our worship."[89] Playing at worship is a half-hearted, shallow effort to curry favor with the Most High. Playing at worship uses vows to manipulate the Creator for one's own ends. This is trifling with the God who alone can empower us to enjoy the gift. When we use worship as a means to an end, we are playing with a "consuming fire" (Heb. 12:29). As my fellow pastor, Daniel Corey, has said, "Worship is the most dangerous thing you do in the course of a week."

A Fool's Sacrifice (5:1–3)

Qoheleth seems aware that just as we may seek success or pleasure to mitigate *hebel* and to have a sense of advantage, we may also try to use God for the same reason. So he writes,

> [1] Guard your steps when you go to the house of God. To draw near to listen is better than to offer the sacrifice of fools, for they do not know that they are doing evil.

> [2] Be not rash with your mouth, nor let your heart be hasty to utter a word before God, for God is in heaven and you are on earth. Therefore, let your words be few.

> [3] For a dream comes with much business, and a fool's voice with many words.

---

[89] Gordon Dahl, *Work, Play, and Worship in a Leisure-Oriented Society* (Minneapolis: Augsburg, 1972), 20.

Going to church? Guard your steps! This is a word of caution to the careless. When you go to worship God, be prepared, be intentional, have a sense of both gravity and gladness. As you enter the doors, realize that what you have to say pales compared to what God has to say. Draw near to listen and listen with care (Luke 8:18). Those who draw near to listen, also draw near to learn and to obey.

The fool bounces into the house of worship holding a lamb on the end of rope with one hand and his cell phone with the other. As he strolls into the house of God, he scrolls through the latest social media posts while thinking that he is performing his duty and that God will bless him. Qoheleth says, "He does not know that he is doing evil." It never occurs to him that God is not a commodity to be used. It never occurs to him he is about to meet the King of the universe.

Qoheleth's warnings continue, "Be not rash with your mouth, nor let your heart be hasty to utter a word before God, for God is in heaven and you are on earth. Therefore, let your words be few" (5:2). What a warning, especially when we consider that we are busy people, with a lot going on, and we are easily distracted. The warning is to make sure that we give our utmost attention to the God we worship. We must be intentional and careful as we pray, sing, and respond to the Word. Being hasty in word and impulsive in thought is a clear demonstration that we are not thinking about the glorious One we have come to worship.

When Qoheleth says, "For God is in heaven and you are on earth," this should not be construed to mean that God is distant but simply that He is God. We are dust, we are mere human beings, we are sinners. God is God, exalted and transcendent. The fool pours out words in worship; the wise man ponders what he hears. The wise man is there is to listen, not to blab. The wisdom of James 1:19 certainly applies: we should be quick to hear and slow to speak. This is not a call to walk silently into church with some kind of pious quietude, but it is a call to take worship seriously and prepare one's heart and mind. It is a call to stand in awe of the Creator/creature distinction.

The next verse is difficult but explains the problem. "For a dream comes with much business, and a fool's voice with many words." The NET and the NLT help us here. "Just as dreams come when there are many cares, so the rash vow of a fool occurs when there are many words" (Eccl. 5:3 NET). "Too much activity gives you restless dreams; too many words make you a fool" (5:3 NLT). The mind wanders (dreams) because it is preoccupied with its own business. Then it produces hurried words, hasty words, impulsive words, to get through the ritual and get on with business. This is not the way to come before God. This is no way to worship. Being distracted or preoccupied with our own business and trying to get in and get out so we can say we satisfied our duty with God is an insult to the King of heaven.[90]

A Dangerous Game (5:4–7)

[4] When you vow a vow to God, do not delay paying it, for he has no pleasure in fools. Pay what you vow.

[5] It is better that you should not vow than that you should vow and not pay.

[6] Let not your mouth lead you into sin, and do not say before the messenger that it was a mistake. Why should God be angry at your voice and destroy the work of your hands?

[7] For when dreams increase and words grow many, there is vanity; but God is the one you must fear.

Qoheleth now tells us that when we make a vow to God, we must not be late in paying it (Eccl. 5:4). The connection is clearly to many hasty words. Making a vow is an act of worship. Vows could be an act of devoting something to God, abstaining

---

[90] Wandering thoughts during worship was a common problem that the Puritans addressed. See Richard Steele, *A Remedy for Wandering Thoughts in Worship* (Harrisonburg, VA: Sprinkle, 1988); Nathaniel Vincent, *Attending Upon God with Distraction* (Grand Rapids: Soli Deo Gloria, 2010).

from something for God, making promises to God, or offering something to God because of his special help. When we make such a dedication, we need to take our words seriously and keep our word. God takes no pleasure in fools who spout an abundance of words. "Bless me Lord, and I will pitch a little extra in the offering. Bless me Lord and I will serve in the nursery or at least 5th and 6th grade boys Sunday School." Don't play games with God. "Instant readiness is the best proof of sincerity."[91] It is better to not make resolutions, promises, covenants, or vows, than to make such commitments and then not follow through. "To refuse to enlist may be guiltless; but to desert the colors is to be guilty of death."[92] To say to the priest, when he shows up to collect, "It was a mistake," is indeed a big mistake!

God is not mocked. If we trifle with Him, if we play at our worship, it will provoke the Lord and there will be consequences (5:6b). "For when dreams increase and words grow many, there is vanity; but God is the one you must fear" (5:7). Kidner says, "The dreams appear to be daydreams, reducing worship to verbal doodling."[93] The words and dreams are a vapor. The remedy to the sacrifice of fools, the cure to trifling with God, is to fear God. An acute awareness of His holiness will cause us to come before Him in reverence and awe. Our God is worthy of our undivided hearts, undivided worship, and listening with all our heart, with a determination to obey. David Gibson remarks, "When I live with the reality of God, the God in heaven who has my heart open before him like an open book, I stand in awe of him, and this takes concrete form in the kind of words that do and do not leave my mouth."[94]

One of the many banes of our contemporary church culture is that worship has been turned into entertainment and God is belittled. Years ago, my wife and I were in a young marrieds

---

[91] Charles Bridges, *Ecclesiastes*, Geneva Series of Commentaries, (Edinburgh: Banner of Truth Trust, 1992), 107.

[92] Bridges, *Ecclesiastes*, 107.

[93] Kidner, *The Message of Ecclesiastes*, 53.

[94] Gibson, *Living Life Backwards*, 88.

Sunday school class and the leader got up and clapped his hands together and said, "All right, let's go to the God who is large and in charge." I wondered if fire was going to come down from heaven. What often passes for worship lacks gravity because it lacks a biblical vision of God. What often passes for joy is nothing more than light-hearted laughter at a silly joke. C. S. Lewis said, "There is a kind of happiness and wonder that makes you serious. It is too good to waste on jokes."[95]

God is the fountain of all our joy. He is the One who gives us the capacity to enjoy the good gifts He has given. We should experience both gladness and gravity in His presence, both joy and awe. But coming into His presence is a dangerous thing. It is dangerous to think that we can use God to get more gifts or get more joy. It is dangerous to be in His presence and think what we have to say is more important than what He has to say. We should prepare our steps that bring us into His presence. We should be prepared to listen. Playing at our worship will not only fail to satisfy our souls, but it will also endanger our souls.

As we prepare our hearts for worship, let us remember we are coming to the living God, who is a consuming fire (Heb. 12:29). Let us remember we are coming to hear the living Word of God (4:12). Let us remember why we can come to God and hear His Word: "Therefore, brothers, since we have confidence to enter the holy places by the blood of Jesus, by the new and living way that he opened for us through the curtain, that is, through his flesh, and since we have a great priest over the house of God, let us draw near with a true heart in full assurance of faith, with our hearts sprinkled clean from an evil conscience and our bodies washed with pure water" (Heb. 10:19–22).

---

[95] C. S. Lewis, *The Last Battle* (New York, NY: Harper Trophy, 1956), 212.

7

Rain on Life's Parade
(5:8–20)

Our hearts should ache over the injustice and oppression that exists in this death row cell under the sun. The vandalism of shalom should unsettle us. Such vandalism seems to pose a threat to God's beautiful plan and a challenge to our joy. But nothing gets past our God. Nothing escapes His notice. Although we should fight against injustice and oppression, we know that it too is *hebel* and justice is coming. But there are self-imposed challenges to enjoying life and labor as a gift. Those challenges are envy (4:4–6), loneliness (4:7–12), and politics (4:13–16). We could also add that careless and shallow worship not only trivializes the enjoyment of the gift, but it also endangers the soul (5:1–7). Trying to use God will not only fail to satisfy our souls but will endanger our souls. Qoheleth now continues to expose more challenges.

Challenge Six: Greed in High Place (5:8–9)

> ⁸ If you see in a province the oppression of the poor and the violation of justice and righteousness, do not be amazed at the matter, for the high official is watched by a higher, and there are yet higher ones over them.

⁹ But this is gain for a land in every way: a king committed to cultivated fields.

Qoheleth returns to the themes of oppression and injustice, which in this instance, is brought about by bureaucrats, kings, politicians, and those holding office. His first counsel is not to be shocked. It is human nature to be self-serving and devour others, like beasts, for personal gain. The problem is truly systemic. This is "graft" in high places. Graft is using one's position, often public office, to obtain personal profit or advantage, through fraud or deceit. It is systemic because each level of the system has its own corruption. "The mere existence of many levels of government administered by many officials makes at least some corruption inevitable."[96]

What can be done? Qoheleth admits not a whole lot can be done. The little guy, contrary to the movies, rarely ever wins. Why? Each parasite protects the parasite beneath him so that the self-serving food chain is not disrupted. What do we expect in a fallen world? How many times have we heard that a story is breaking that will expose some terrible corruption? How many times do those stories result in anyone being caught, let alone imprisoned?

Verse 9 is challenging since there are several possible translations. The translations basically fall into two categories. These are that either the despotic government serves a purpose or that the government always steals, even the king. Both the ESV and NASB go in the direction that a king (in the context, the one who is on top of this devouring food chain), at least keeps the fields cultivated. Government may be evil, but it is a necessary evil.[97] "The writer is sensitive to oppression (5:8) but does not hold that anarchy or violent revolution is a viable alternative."[98]

---

[96] Garrett, *Proverbs, Ecclesiastes, Song of Songs*, 312.
[97] Garrett, *Proverbs, Ecclesiastes, Song of Songs*, 312.
[98] Eaton, *Ecclesiastes*, 117.

The other view is that the government always steals, even the king, is reflected in a few translations.

> "The profit from the land is taken by all; the king is served by the field" (CSB).

> "The produce of the land is seized by all of them, even the king is served by the fields" (NET).

> "The increase from the land is taken by all; the king himself profits from the fields" (NIV).

> "The phrase means that all the officials, from the king on down, take a portion of the profits from the farmer's field."[99]

Whichever one is correct, we cannot lose sight of the gift, nor can we lose sight of God's sovereignty. God appoints kings and those in authority, and although never an excuse for oppression or injustice, it will also be God who judges. When we see people in positions of power abusing that power, we can do what we can, but at the end of the day, under the sun, the bad guy usually wins. Bad kings and elected officials take advantage of their office and those under them are the ones who suffer. But nothing gets past God.

Challenge Seven: The Love of Money (5:10–12)

If anything threatens our capacity to enjoy the gifts of God, it is to love the gift more than the Giver.

> [10] He who loves money will not be satisfied with money, nor he who loves wealth with his income; this also is vanity.

> [11] When goods increase, they increase who eat them, and what advantage has their owner but to see them with his eyes?

> [12] Sweet is the sleep of a laborer, whether he eats little or much, but the full stomach of the rich will not let him sleep.

---

[99] Farmer, *Proverbs and Ecclesiastes*, 168.

The disease of loving money has several disastrous side effects. The person who loves money will never be satisfied with money. Money cannot satisfy because it is a vapor. Money is a gift from God to be used wisely and enjoyed, but the minute we try to get more out of money than God designed, we ruin the gift. The apostle Paul will warn, "But those who desire to be rich fall into temptation, into a snare, into many senseless and harmful desires that plunge people into ruin and destruction. For the love of money is a root of all kinds of evils. It is through this craving that some have wandered away from the faith and pierced themselves with many pangs" (1 Tim. 6:9–10).

Another nasty side effect is that those who love money attract leeches. When the love of money begins to "pay off" and "goods increase," so do the freeloaders. "The poor is disliked even by his neighbor, but the rich has many friends" (Prov. 14:20). "Wealth brings many new friends, but a poor man is deserted by his friend" (19:4). These friends are not friends at all. They don't love the money-loving rich guy. They are just money-loving barnacles that attach to his ship, and all he can do is look on.

Insomnia is another side effect of making money an idolatrous mistress. The working man is content with what God gives. The working man, the one who sees his labor and his rest as divine gifts, drifts off to sleep easily. Even if he has a hunger pang or two, he has a good conscience, a healthy view of life, and his sleep is pleasant. The rich man, on the other hand, lays in bed, tossing and turning. Anxiety robs him of sleep, as he lays there worrying about either gaining more or losing what he has. He would write a big check to pay for a good night's sleep, but money can't buy a sound night's sleep.

Challenge Eight: Money Gained, Money Gone (5:13–17)

Qoheleth frequently talks about money. It is an important part of life. It can be a gift from God. But the wrong attitude towards money will ruin us. Qoheleth now moves to a "grievous evil that

I have seen under the sun."

> ¹³ Riches were kept by their owner to his hurt,
>
> 14 and those riches were lost in a bad venture. And he is father of a son, but he has nothing in his hand.
>
> ¹⁵ As he came from his mother's womb he shall go again, naked as he came, and shall take nothing for his toil that he may carry away in his hand.
>
> ¹⁶ This also is a grievous evil: just as he came, so shall he go, and what gain is there to him who toils for the wind?
>
> ¹⁷ Moreover, all his days he eats in darkness in much vexation and sickness and anger.

The portrait Qoheleth paints for us is of a man who hoards riches to his own hurt. This man works and saves. He then takes the sizeable sum, representing his toil and sacrificial saving, and then loses it through a bad investment. This man had a goal of wanting to leave something for his son, and he lost it through unfortunate turns of events. The riches hoarded did not benefit the intended beneficiary. Under such a frowning providence, the money which was believed to secure a son's future grew wings and flew away (Prov. 23:4–5). There is a strong echo of Job's statement, "Naked I came from my mother's womb, and naked shall I return. The LORD gave, and the LORD has taken away; blessed be the name of the LORD." However, here in Ecclesiastes, "blessed be the name of the LORD" seems conspicuously absent.

The man has nothing to show for the overtime. Nothing to show for the savings. Nothing to show for the investment. All he has is the sadness of this "grievous evil." He eats in darkness, that is, in misery, isolation, sickness, and anger (Eccl. 5:17). The resentments of a lost future give birth to anger which eats away every little bit of joy. The problem wasn't hard work, saving, or investing; the problem was thinking that he could secure the future with money. The desire to secure a son's future is a good desire. As Solomon says elsewhere, "A good man leaves an inheritance to his children's children" (Prov. 13:22). The problem, as Paul puts it, is that it involves setting our hopes on the "uncertainty of riches" (1 Tim. 6:17). So, what shall we do? Shall we live in poverty? Refuse to plan?

Man's Lot in Life (5:18–20)

As the ride bumps along, Qoheleth mercifully gives us a little reprieve. He revisits the remedy; he reminds us of the corner pieces of the puzzle.

> [18] Behold, what I have seen to be good and fitting is to eat and drink and find enjoyment in all the toil with which one toils under the sun the few days of his life that God has given him, for this is his lot.
>
> [19] Everyone also to whom God has given wealth and possessions and power to enjoy them, and to accept his lot and rejoice in his toil—this is the gift of God.
>
> [20] For he will not much remember the days of his life because God keeps him occupied with joy in his heart.

Qoheleth steps forward and says, "Yes, there is much misery and darkness in this life under the sun, but I have seen the good and the beautiful." It is significant that he uses the word "beautiful" (ESV, "fitting") because it hearkens back to 3:11, which said, "He is making all things beautiful in his time." Part of God's good plan is that in a world of vexation, sickness, and anger, there is the good and beautiful. Each of us can (and must) still eat and drink and find enjoyment in the hard work that God has given us to do. It is the life of faith and joy that lays hold of the brevity of life and sees it as a precious gift given by God that will soon be past (1 Tim. 6:17). The things of earth, the mundane, eating, drinking, and working, constitute God's reward to us.

The power to enjoy the gifts is also a gift (Eccl. 5:19). The way to avoid living in the darkness is to embrace life and all that it entails as a gift. If God takes part of it away, we are not reduced to eating in darkness, battling ulcers and anxiety, and suppressed anger. Instead, we can say, "The LORD gave, the LORD took away, blessed be the name of the LORD" (Job 1:21). God is the source of whatever wealth we possess (Deut. 8:18; Prov. 10:22). God is also the One who determined the "when" of wealth. He can give it. He can take it away. He can restore it, sustain it, increase it, or make it fly off never to be seen again. The power to receive it as a gift and then hold it loosely is also a gift.

The busyness of achievement for personal gain is misery. To be preoccupied with the pursuit for the sake of pursuit will suck joy out of life, give sleepless nights, and add grief upon grief. If anything can slow down life, it is misery. But the life that is enjoyed will go by quickly. The happier and more content we are, the more occupied we will be with the joys of life, and the more quickly it will pass by. But we should not want to trade the vapor of happiness in God for anything. So, enjoy the gifts but hold them loosely. Love the Giver more than the gifts, because when the gift goes away, the Giver remains.

8

Life without a Can Opener
(6:1–12)

Why so much emphasis on money and work? Work is a major part of life. Earning money through labor is one of the primary reasons we work. Work is a gift. Money is a gift. God provides through the gift. However, both money and work are easily spoiled by expecting more from them than they can give. Qoheleth knows truth which impacts and shapes life does not come easily or quickly. It's not learned the first time around. Worldviews are formed through repetition, not one lecture. Truth must be kneaded into our hearts and minds. Although this chapter seems like a downer, Qoheleth is beating the truth into our heads. He does not want us to spoil the gifts of work and money. He does not want us to waste our breath.

Satisfaction NOT Guaranteed (6:1–6)

In chapter six, we encounter one of Qoheleth's hypothetical yet all too common characters. This person has everything: wealth, possessions, and children. Then he dies. What is missing in his outwardly blessed life is the ability to enjoy the blessings.

> ¹ There is an evil that I have seen under the sun, and it lies heavy on mankind:
>
> ² a man to whom God gives wealth, possessions, and

honor, so that he lacks nothing of all that he desires, yet God does not give him power to enjoy them, but a stranger enjoys them. This is vanity; it is a grievous evil.

³ If a man fathers a hundred children and lives many years, so that the days of his years are many, but his soul is not satisfied with life's good things, and he also has no burial, I say that a stillborn child is better off than he.

⁴ For it comes in vanity and goes in darkness, and in darkness its name is covered.

⁵ Moreover, it has not seen the sun or known anything, yet it finds rest rather than he.

⁶ Even though he should live a thousand years twice over, yet enjoy no good—do not all go to the one place?

The prevalent evil in view is as overwhelming as it is common. God gives a man everything. This man lacks nothing. He not only has everything he needs but everything he desires. But one thing is missing, and it is that God has not granted him the grace to enjoy the abundance. Instead, a foreigner, not a family member, who did not work for any of it, enjoys it all. Qoheleth examines this situation and concludes it is *hebel* and a severe affliction. Sometimes the mere breath is just a breath, but when it is compounded with affliction, it is a grievous evil. This *hebel* weighs heavy on mankind. What advantage has the man to whom God has given everything and yet not the grace to enjoy it? Nothing. Absolutely nothing.

Qoheleth presents another hypothetical figure: a man who fathers a hundred children and lives many years. A multitude of children and long life are both signs of divine blessing (Deut. 4:40; Ps. 127:3–5). But if he isn't satisfied with God's good gifts and then dies without even getting a headstone, Qoheleth says it is better if he never lived. With one hundred kids and lots of friends, surely someone would have buried this man who couldn't "get no satisfaction." A decent burial was the fitting last chapter of a blessed life. No burial would have been a disgrace. Having no funeral would have been worse than nobody showing up to your funeral! Not one of the hundred kids came by to pick up the body. None of the leeches showed any gratitude and took his corpse from the morgue to the cemetery. Riches, honor, and external blessing were his, but he lacked the ability to enjoy it and then suffered dishonor in the end. What *hebel*! What a "grievous ill." There is much more to life than outward blessings.

The stillborn, who is better off than the man who could not enjoy God's gifts, is now described. The child comes in a vapor, goes out in darkness, and in darkness his or her name is covered with obscurity. "The *name* in Hebrew thought is more than a label; it includes the personality and the character. The still born has no chance to develop a character or acquire a reputation."[100] The stillborn never sees the sun, that is, never has a chance to enjoy life. But the stillborn is still better off than our guy in Ecclesiastes 6:1–3 because at least the stillborn finds rest.

Now Qoheleth, in a hyperbolic flourish, says even if the rich guy lives a millennium, twice, he still goes to the same place as the stillborn. One thousand years would be the perfect life. Even if this rich man has two perfect lives with all his blessings, he still dies. "It is the *quality* of life to which Qoheleth is referring, not its duration. If one is denied enjoying one's life, then one is better off never entering the world at all."[101]   There is no inextricable link between prosperity and   God's favor. This smashes the conventional paradigm. This scenario is fingernails on a chalkboard. If money, lots of kids, and a long life are blessings, doesn't that mean the rich man is on good ground with God? Qoheleth gives a resounding no! The rich guy might have a warehouse stocked full of cans of peaches, but if he doesn't even have a Swiss Army Knife can opener, he is to be pitied.

---

[100] Eaton, *Ecclesiastes*, 106.

[101] Ogden, *Qoheleth*, 91, italics original.

A graceless man with a big bank account and a full quiver is the picture of sadness.

Full, But Still Hungry (6:7–9)

> [7] All the toil of man is for his mouth, yet his appetite is not satisfied.
>
> [8] For what advantage has the wise man over the fool? And what does the poor man have who knows how to conduct himself before the living?
>
> [9] Better is the sight of the eyes than the wandering of the appetite: this also is vanity and a striving after wind.

We work to eat and eat to work. But working is never what ultimately satisfies the appetite. This section serves as a summary and underscores the truth that if life is reduced to working to eat and eating to work, it will leave us unfulfilled. As Qoheleth points this out, one might imagine a rabbi who is listening say, "Qoheleth, true enough. But you are forgetting wisdom! Don't forget wisdom." Qoheleth retorts, "Of course I value wisdom, but let's not overplay that hand. In the end, neither wisdom, nor even social skills, are guaranteed to pay off."

Qoheleth then turns to sight. Qoheleth never gives up on wisdom because wisdom is always better. Here he refers to wisdom as "seeing eyes" since they express the ability to perceive and enjoy life. Having that sight is better than wandering appetites. The continual motion, the fluctuations, and the vacillations, driven by desire, are never satisfied. The wise have a fixed gaze, firm priorities, a perspective on life and the grace to enjoy it. The wandering heart of unfulfilled appetites drives to and fro. Qoheleth then concedes, but this too is *hebel* and chasing the wind. Both the seeing eyes and wandering desire are a vapor. So although wisdom is better, it still doesn't resolve *hebel*.

Boxing with God (6:10–12)

[10] Whatever has come to be has already been named, and it is known what man is, and that he is not able to dispute with one stronger than he.

[11] The more words, the more vanity, and what is the advantage to man?

[12] For who knows what is good for man while he lives the few days of his vain life, which he passes like a shadow? For who can tell man what will be after him under the sun.

This final paragraph serves as a hinge verse between the first part of the book and the second. He first notes that "whatever has come to be has already been named." By this he means that things in this life are settled. The nature of man is unambiguous: he is a breath, a beast, and profoundly limited. Our ability to dispute with God over any of this is an illusion. Our arms are far too short to box with God. "Man cannot escape his limitations, nor can he completely unravel the world's anomalies (cf. 1:15). He may, like Job, wish to debate the matter with God, but God is altogether greater."[102] Our arguments, our retorts, our rebuttals are a vapor. Or as the NET puts it, "The more one argues with words, the less he accomplishes. How does that benefit him?" (6:11). This verse reminds us that talking, arguing, and debating, will change nothing. We are slow to realize this and the multitude of armchair philosophers and theologians, along with a few lawyers, railing against God only pile up the *hebel*. A mountain of vapors is still a vapor.

The final verse is one that clearly demonstrates *hebel* is not futility or meaningless. This verse tells us that we have only a few days and that we spend them like a shadow. In these few days, who knows what is good? The sage of Ecclesiastes has already answered this question (2:24–26; 3:12; 5:18). The wise man who knows God knows what is good. The good is to see life as a gift,

---

[102] Eaton, *Ecclesiastes*, 123.

enjoy it as a gift, and then leave what comes after to God. You don't know the future, so trust God.

This passage is a dark part of the forest, and it reminds us that we are a moment, but God is eternal. We are a vapor, but God is forever. We are limited; God is without measure. The fulfillment we long for is not in the money we earn or the achievements of a career. A happy life is not found in just a little bit more. As Qoheleth brings this leg of the ride to an end through a dark tunnel, he reminds us to enjoy life as God has given it to us. If we don't, it would have been better for us never to have been born. Indeed, as Jeremy Taylor warned long ago, "God threatens terrible things if we will not be happy."[103]

---

[103] Quoted by John Piper, *Desiring God*, rev. ed. (Colorado Springs, CO: Multnomah, 2011), 9.

9

Your Better Life Now
(7:1–12)

From the looks of it, people are happier than ever. Social media accounts seem to indicate that most of us are living our best lives right now. Our lives, as reflected on our social media accounts, appear to be full of thrilling vacations, cute puppies, exotic cuisine, successful fat-burning workouts, new purchases, family bliss, and of course, selfies upon selfies. However, we know better. That best life exists only on a computer screen. From Qoheleth's perspective, the problem with thinking that this is our best life now is that death is going to have the last word. Not even a postmortem Facebook post can soften the blow of the reality of death. Death simply ruins the "best life now mentality." Is there a better way than to scratch and scrape to try to have your best life now? Qoheleth will tell us there is no best life now; death ruins that dream. But it is possible, looking at life backwards, to live a good life now. The word we see repeatedly translated, "better," is simply "good." Living our good life now means living by wisdom, embracing this short life as a gift from God, and enjoying each fleeting chapter. This kind of good life is better than all the attempts at one's "best life now."

Qoheleth changes his style in chapter 7, but he does not change his provocative spirit. The first six chapters are full of reflections, arguments, questions, deductions, and conclusions. Now he is going to "bombard us with proverbs."[104] The proverbs he writes fit into the category of "better" proverbs. There are no less than twenty-three "better" proverbs in the book of Proverbs.[105] A few examples are in order:

> "Better is a little with the fear of the LORD than great treasure and trouble with it.
>
> Better is a dinner of herbs where love is than a fattened ox and hatred with it" (Prov. 15:16–17).
>
> "Better is a dry morsel with quiet than a house full of feasting with strife" (17:1).
>
> "It is better to live in a corner of the housetop than in a house shared with a quarrelsome wife" (21:9).
>
> "It is better to live in a desert land than with a quarrelsome and fretful woman" (21:19).

There are also twenty-three "better" statements in Qoheleth. Chapter 7 gives us a series of them. They compare two things and state what is "good," or by way of comparison, what is "better." They show the way of wisdom, and that way sets before us our better life now.

Lessons Learned from the Funeral (7:1–4)

> [1] A good name is better than precious ointment,
> and the day of death than the day of birth.
>
> [2] It is better to go to the house of mourning
> than to go to the house of feasting,
> for this is the end of all mankind,
> and the living will lay it to heart.
>
> [3] Sorrow is better than laughter,
> for by sadness of face the heart is made glad.

---

[104] Kidner, *The Message of Ecclesiastes*, 64.

[105] The "better" Proverbs also use the word "good" in a comparative sense, thus the translation, "better."

> [4] The heart of the wise is in the house of mourning,
> but the heart of fools is in the house of mirth.

The first proverb deals with one's character. A good reputation is better than lots of perfume. Perfume, in the ancient world, covered up bad smells. A good reputation reflects one's inner character and it does not require hiding or covering over something bad or unpleasant. This first proverb is not disconnected from what follows. "The day of one's death is better than the day of one's birth." This seems awfully morbid. But as David Gibson notes, "In my opinion, the Preacher is saying that the day of your death is a better teacher than the day of your birth.... A coffin preaches better sermons than a cot [i.e., a crib]."[106]

Qoheleth continues this line of thought that death is a good teacher when he tells us, "It is better to go to the house of mourning than to go to the house of feasting, because that is the end of every man, and the living will lay it to heart." For the living, it is better to go to a funeral than to a party. Qoheleth did not say it was more fun to go to the funeral than to the party but that it was "better." Indeed, the coffin is a better teacher than rowdy laughter. The wise person attends the funeral, and he reflects on his own death. He thinks about the reputation he will leave behind. He thinks about the words that will be spoken about him. "Will they need a vat of perfume to cover up the stench of my character, or will they be able to speak with a good conscience?" He thinks about the reality that one day he will breathe his last. "Every funeral anticipates our own."[107]

On Boothill, the famous graveyard outside of Tombstone, Arizona, there is a grave marker that Qoheleth would have approved:

---

[106] Gibson, *Living Life Backwards*, 96. "Cot" can refer to a "crib" among the Scottish.
[107] Eaton, *Ecclesiastes*, 109.

As you pass by
Remember that as
You are so once was I
And as I am you
Soon will be
Remember me

"Sorrow is better than laughter, for by sadness of face the heart is made glad" (Eccl. 7:3). Qoheleth is not discounting laughter. There is a time to laugh (3:4). But for the mind that reflects on death, there is sobriety, even sorrow, that cannot disappear with a joke. Nevertheless, don't think that this sorrow is a hopeless one, for there can be a deeper happiness in the heart even when the heart is sad. This gladness can run deep because living life from the perspective of death compels us to see it as a breath and a gift to be enjoyed while we have it. This is why the heart of the wise does not mind spending time in the house of mourning (7:4a), but the heart of the fool only thinks about having a good time (7:4b). The wise man ponders while he is at the funeral, and he learns. The fool avoids the funeral, and parties like it is 1999.[108]

To live the good life now, we need to let death be our teacher. We need to reflect on the end of our own lives. We need the wisdom that only our own impending deaths can give us. The death of others and the prospect of our own should cause us to think about how we live today so when people gather at our funeral, we won't need vats of perfume to mask a poor character and stained reputation.

The Song of Fools (7:5–6)

⁵ It is better for a man to hear the rebuke of the wise than to hear the song of fools.

⁶ For as the crackling of thorns under a pot,

---

[108] For those old enough to remember, this is a reference to Prince's song "1999." See, Prince, "1999," track 1 on 1999, Warner Bros., 1982.

> so is the laughter of the fools;
> this also is vanity.

If we are to live the good life, we need to be wise enough to receive rebukes from the wise. The fool wants to be entertained, the wise man wants to learn, even if it is unpleasant. Just as sorrow proves more profitable than laughter and the house of mourning is better than the house of feasting, so the stinging words of rebuke are better than the superficial song that comes from a fool. "If given a choice between hearing a wise man enumerate your faults and hearing the Spice Girls try to sing something, the choice is an easy one."[109] "A scoffer does not like to be reproved; he will not go to the wise" (Prov. 15:12). "The ear that listens to life-giving reproof will dwell among the wise" (15:31).

The next picture in Ecclesiastes 7:6 is vivid: "For as the crackling of thorns under a pot, so is the laughter of the fools; this also is vanity." When thorn bushes are burned, they are loud. There are plenty of snaps, crackles, and pops, but in terms of fuel, they are worthless. They burn loudly but are consumed too quickly to be useful under a pot. The fool's response to rebuke is carnal laughter at the wise man. He scoffs and laughs off the rebuke, but his response is useless and a vapor. His songs and his laughter are vapors that reflect his superficial attitude toward the serious things of life.

The Corrupt Heart (7:7)

> [7] Surely oppression drives the wise into madness,
> and a bribe corrupts the heart.

The NIV captures the meaning of verse 7: "Extortion turns a wise person into a fool, and a bribe corrupts the heart." Extortion robs a man of his reason.[110] Extortion and bribery are not only short-sighted, but also corrupting, corrosive behaviors

---

[109] Wilson, *Joy at the End of the Tether*, 78. Realizing this reference is somewhat dated, please replace the Spice Girls with Taylor Swift or whoever the latest female pop singer happens to be.

[110] The Tanakh (JPS) translation of Ecclesiastes 7:7 supports the idea that extortion robs a man of his reason. It reads, "For cheating may rob the wise man of reason."

that undermine one's good name and overthrow his wisdom. This path of oppression for self-gain is a bog of iniquity that pulls the oppressor down deeper and deeper. The fog of sin increasingly clouds one's judgment. The wise man must remain firm in his uprightness and maintain his integrity. Any other path brings about the corruption of his character.

Anger's Lodge (7:8–9)

> [8] Better is the end of a thing than its beginning, and the patient in spirit is better than the proud in spirit.
> [9] Be not quick in your spirit to become angry, for anger lodges in the bosom of fools.

The next proverb is a couplet and says, "The end of a matter is better than its beginning; Patience of spirit is better than haughtiness of spirit" (Eccl. 7:8, NASB). Seeing something through, finishing a task, is the path of wisdom. When one sets a goal and then accomplishes that goal, there is a sense of satisfaction. Any fool can start a thousand projects, but completion and fulfillment demonstrate wisdom. Furthermore, the end of a trial is better than its beginning. When a trial or ordeal makes its appearance, there are dark foreboding clouds. The sun ceases to shine. But as those trials see the beginning of the end, the sun starts to peek through the clouds again. There were lessons learned and the end was better than the beginning. "It is good for me that I was afflicted, that I might learn your statutes" (Ps. 119:71).

Whether it is a task or a trial, patience is required to persevere. The patient person knows he or she is not in control. They cannot manipulate or expedite the outcome. The humble rest. The proud rage. The proud person is the impatient person. Their impatience is driven by believing that what they want, they want now. The haughty of spirit are entitled. They believe everyone and everything exists to serve them. Irritability is one of the ugly fruits of pride. This heart attitude mistreats people because they are not people but impediments. The wise man is the patient man.

In addition to patience, the wise man also is one who shuns anger. Verse 9 is a warning against being eager or hasty to be angry. Some people walk through this life eager to be angry. We say, "They have a hair-trigger." They thrive on being angry. Anger is food for their twisted heart. Anger finds a welcome home in the heart of a fool. "There it resides, there it remains, there it has the innermost and uppermost place, there it is hugged as that which is dear, and laid in the bosom, and not easily parted with."[111]

"The Good Old Days" (7:10)

> [10] Say not, "Why were the former days better than these?" For it is not from wisdom that you ask this.

Wisdom does not long for the good old days. We are romantics when it comes to the good old days. To be sure, there is nothing wrong with looking back with fondness on bygone eras, but if there is nothing new under the sun, then there is no such thing as the good old days. Every day, every era, has its strengths, its weaknesses, its virtues, and its vices. The folly comes when we think the former days were just better than our days. Qoheleth says such a romanticized view of the past does not come from wisdom. I think Qoheleth would have smirked or outright laughed at this country song from 1986.

> Grandpa, tell me 'bout the good old days
> Sometimes it feels like this world's gone crazy
> Grandpa, take me back to yesterday
> When the line between right and wrong
> Didn't seem so hazy
> Did lovers really fall in love to stay
> And stand beside each other, come what may
> Was a promise really something people kept
> Not just something they would say
> Did families really bow their heads to pray

---

[111] Matthew Henry, *Matthew Henry's Commentary on the Whole Bible: Complete and Un-abridged in One Volume* (Peabody: Hendrickson, 1994), 1043.

> Did daddies really never go away
> Oh, grandpa, tell me 'bout the good old days
> Grandpa, everything is changing fast
> We call it progress, but I just don't know
> And grandpa, let's wander back into the past
> And paint me the picture of long ago.[112]

What about the happy days of yesteryear? If life is a vapor, don't waste it by bemoaning that life isn't like your childhood. Wisdom refuses to idolize the past in order to dismiss the present. "Often when we ask this, it's because we are blind to the good things of the present and ignorant of the evil of the past."[113] Wisdom may evaluate the times, but it doesn't cripple itself with endless questions about the good old days and why can't today be like it was in 1977? Such thinking leaves God out of the equation and turns a blind eye to the troubles of the past and the blessings of the present.

If You've Got the Money (7:11–12)

> [11] Wisdom is good with an inheritance, an advantage to those who see the sun.

> [12] For the protection of wisdom is like the protection of money, and the advantage of knowledge is that wisdom preserves the life of him who has it.

Wisdom also has benefits for the good life, especially if there is some money to go along with it. Certainly, money does not ultimately satisfy, and it definitely does not mitigate *hebel*, as Qoheleth has already painfully expounded. But wisdom with some money is preferable to folly and poverty. Both wisdom and money can offer temporary protection in a tough life, but in the final analysis, wisdom is better than money.

---

[112] Jamie O'Hara, "Grandpa (Tell Me 'Bout the Good Old Days)," track 2 on *Rockin' with the Rhythm*, RCA Nashville/Curb, 1986.

[113] Gibson, *Living Life Backwards*, 102.

Conclusion

Every one of us will eventually have our run in with the King of Terrors. We should really learn from him a thing or two. First and foremost, we need to remember that Jesus defeated death, and death does not have the last word. Jesus has taken the sting out of death through His death and resurrection. So we sing,

> No fear in life, no guilt in death,
> this is the power of Christ in me,
> from life's first cry to final breath,
> Jesus commands my destiny.[114]

Yes and amen! But let's keep in mind that although our future with the Lord is our ultimate hope, this short life is a precious gift. Perhaps we can take our cue from Joe Rigney's book, *Strangely Bright*.[115] The title plays off the Gospel hymn, "Turn your eyes upon Jesus, look full in his wonderful face, and the things of earth will grow strangely dim, in the light of his glory and grace."[116] Rigney persuasively argues that when we turn our eyes on Jesus, the things of earth grow strangely bright in the light of His glory and grace.

Since this is not our best life and that life is still to come, what makes this vapor brighter? Choosing the good, choosing the better, choosing wisdom, which means I ponder my end. I receive correction. I avoid corruption and anger. I refuse to be crippled by pining for the good old days. I am thankful if I have some money and use it wisely. I live this short life with the wisdom that says, "One day I will die," so I seek to live life in a way that when family and friends gather at my funeral, there will be much to give thanks to God for. It is only when we take our own death seriously that we are able to live today's vapor with joy.

---

[114] Keith and Kristyn Getty, "In Christ Alone," track 7 on *In Christ Alone*, Getty Music, 2006.

[115] Joe Rigney, *Strangely Bright: Can You Love God and Enjoy This World?* (Wheaton, IL: Crossway, 2020).

[116] These words were originally penned by Helen Howarth Lemmel and published in 1918. She entitled the song "The Heavenly Vision," and it is also known by the first line of its refrain, which is, "Turn your eyes upon Jesus."

It is as we consider our days, and consider our end, that we live the good life now.

10

God of My Good
Days and Bad
(7:13–15)

None of us knows what the future holds. None of us knows what will happen an hour from now, let alone tomorrow. Qoheleth has hammered us with this truth: God knows, we don't. But what if my good days give way to bad ones? What if things don't turn out the way I want them to? What if a huge disappointment is right around the corner? Vaneetha Risner, in her article, "What If the Worst Happens?" honestly says, "I've spent a lifetime considering the 'what ifs.' Those questions have a way of unsettling me, destroying my peace, leaving me insecure. I wondered: If my health spirals downward and I end up in an institution, will God be enough? If my children rebel and never walk closely with the Lord, will God be enough? If I never remarry and never feel loved again, will God be enough? If my ministry doesn't flourish and I never see fruit from it, will God be enough? If my suffering continues and I never see the purpose in it, will God be enough?"[117]

In this fleeting life, the bad days seem to threaten our joy. If we only have so much time in this short life, what do we do if most of it is filled with the dark clouds of suffering? What if

[117] Vaneetha Risner, "What if the Worst Happens?" Desiring God, 15 September 2014, https://www.desiringgod.org/articles/what-if-the-worst-happens.

my vapor has more than its fair share of "the worst"? Qoheleth understands that the message of "enjoy this short breath" can encounter many obstacles. He exhorts us now to do two things: (1) consider the work of God and (2) accept the work of God.

A Crook in the Lot (7:13–15)

> [13] Consider the work of God: who can make straight what he has made crooked?
>
> [14] In the day of prosperity be joyful, and in the day of adversity consider: God has made the one as well as the other, so that man may not find out anything that will be after him.
>
> [15] In my vain life I have seen everything. There is a righteous man who perishes in his righteousness, and there is a wicked man who prolongs his life in his evildoing.

Throughout this book Qoheleth has been an observer and investigator who considers, ponders, and studies (cf. 1:13, 17; 2:12). In this passage his focus narrows and draws us in to consider the work of God. The wise man has a lens as he looks, and that lens is the work of God, or God's providence. The Westminster Shorter Catechism asks, "Q. 11. What are God's works of providence? A. God's works of providence are, his most holy, wise, and powerful preserving and governing all his creatures, and all their actions." The Heidelberg Catechism puts it more beautifully: "Q. 27. What do you understand by the providence of God? A. God's providence is His almighty and ever-present power, whereby, as with His hand, He still upholds heaven and earth and all creatures, and so governs them that leaf and blade, rain and drought, fruitful and barren years, food and drink, health and sickness, riches and poverty, indeed, all things, come not by chance but by His fatherly hand."

The work of God is His providence over His world and over our lives. Qoheleth says consider His almighty hand in governing the affairs of everything. We might think the natural thing to say next would be, "For everything he does is beautiful." But Qoheleth is not going to go there. Instead, we need to consider God's providence because who can straighten what He has bent? Bent things are the things which seem to be wrong in God's world. We like right angles, straight lines, and symmetry. If we see something bent, we want to straighten it so it will be as it should be. Stuff needs to be straight! But we can't (1:15), and we can't because it is none other than God who has bent it. The Scriptures teach us that God has all power, that He has a perfect, wise, and holy will, and that He rules over all. Job learned this lesson the hard way. "I know that you can do all things, and that no purpose of yours can be thwarted" (Job 42:2).

Prosperity's Prescription: Rejoice! (7:14a)

The next step after "consider" God's work is to "accept" God's work. "In the day of prosperity be happy" (7:14). In the day when everything seems straight, when everything seems good, when things are the way they are supposed to be, be happy. The phrase, "in the day of prosperity" is literally, "in the good day." The phrase, "be joyful" is "be in the good." In the good day, be in the good, that is, enjoy it. There is nothing wrong with enjoying the good days.

There are times when we should sing, "Blessed be Your name, when the sun's shining down on me, when the world's all it should be, blessed be Your name."[118] Yes, when the sun's shining down on us, when the world's as it should be, be happy! Enjoy such days as gifts from God.

Adversity's Answer: Consider (7:14b)

The good days don't stick around forever. The days of prosperity don't last a lifetime. Adversity will come. "In the day of adversity," is literally in the Hebrew text, "in the day of evil." Solomon is referring to the day when the bad stuff happens. If we are

---

[118] Matt and Beth Redman, "Blessed Be Your Name," track 2 on *Where Angels Fear to Tread*, Worship Together, 2002.

thinking, then we might conjecture that Qoheleth's next move is to say this: good days be happy; bad days, be sad, whine, and complain! That would be symmetrical, but not biblical. Rather, he tells us, "In the day of adversity, consider this." When the day of adversity hits us, Qoheleth wants us to think and consider that God has made the good day as well as the bad day. The Bible is not shy in declaring God's sovereignty over everything, even the bad (Isa. 45:7; Lam. 3:38; Amos 3:6). God makes the good days and the bad. "Blessed be Your name, on the road marked with suffering, though there's pain in the offering, blessed be Your name."[119] Reflect on the truth that God makes both days and has a purpose in both. Consider that God knows what He is doing even though you probably don't have a clue. Acknowledge that both days come from His hand.

When Job experienced the worst day of his life, it was like getting hit by ocean wave after ocean wave of unspeakable pain. Satan had claimed that if God stretched out His hand and touched all that Job had, he would curse God to His face (Job 1:9–11). That included his children. God allows Satan to do his worst, and the worst happens (1:12–19). There is a crescendo of suffering: "There came a messenger to Job…. While he was yet speaking, there came another … and another … and another." Job fell on the ground and worshiped (1:20–22). God points out to Satan that Job held fast to his integrity (2:3). Satan then ups the ante, saying, "Stretch out your hand and touch his bone and flesh and he will curse you to your face" (2:5). God turns Job over into Satan's hand with the restriction that he "only spare his life." Job is then hit with further suffering in the form of boils from head to foot. The pain was excruciating (2:7–8). Then Job's next trial comes from an unexpected source—Mrs. Job: "Then his wife said to him, 'Do you still hold fast your integrity? Curse God and die'" (2:9).

It is Job's response that powerfully illustrates Qoheleth's point. "But he said to her, 'You speak as one of the foolish women would speak. Shall we receive good from God, and

---

[119] Redman and Redman, "Blessed Be Your Name."

shall we not receive evil?" In all this Job did not sin with his lips" (2:10). Job understood that both the good day and the day of evil were from the hand of God. He made each of them. Shall we only accept the good and not receive the bad too?

Qoheleth concludes Ecclesiastes 7:14 by saying, "So that man may not find out anything that will be after him." We acknowledge God is over both days. We can't straighten what He has bent, and He also keeps us from knowing what will come after us. Just as in Ecclesiastes 3:1–15, we know He is sovereign, and we know there is a reason, but in the end, we do not know why, and we certainly don't know how all of it will play out after we are gone. Qoheleth is drilling down on our limitations. We do not have the capacity to read providence with clear eyes. We cannot see the future. All we can do is rest in the hands of a good and sovereign God, enjoying this life as a gift, reflecting on Him when He dispenses adversity, and trusting Him in the darkness. When the worst happens, we don't need to know why or what the outcome will be. All we need to know is that God is enough. *"God doesn't promise us a trouble-free life. But he does promise that he will be there in the midst of our sorrows."*[120]

Qoheleth then gives one other note on the work of God. He writes, "In my vain (fleeting) life I have seen everything. There is a righteous man who perishes in his righteousness, and there is a wicked man who prolongs his life in his evildoing" (7:15). There is some debate about whether verse 15 goes with verses 13–14 or verses 16–18. It seems that Qoheleth is saying in his short, vaporous, *not vain*, life, he has seen it all.

What troubles him, for good measure, is one more crooked thing. A righteous man perishes while being righteous and a wicked man prolongs his life in his wickedness. This is not the way things ought to be. But it is a potent reminder to us, who are under His sovereign hand, that we cannot control the good days or the days of adversity by what we do. The wicked, who deserve many bad days, may have very few. The righteous, who

---

[120] Risner, "What if the Worst Happens," italics original.

(we would think) should have more good days than bad, have the ultimate bad day when he perishes. Life does not make sense.

Conclusion

When adversity strikes, what do we do? Do we simply and stoically affirm we believe in divine sovereignty? Do we, with stiff upper lip, accept the divine purpose as if it were a cold, clinical decree? Do we become cynics? This is the way life is, suck it up buttercup?

No to all of these responses! We remember that our sovereign God is not impersonal, but He is near us in the day of adversity (Ps. 34:18). He is good, He is faithful, and He is kind. In the day of adversity, how do we know those things are true of Him? We know that because in our own evil, in our own self-imposed sin and miserable rebellion, God entered in this world, my world, through His Son. The Lord Jesus Christ paid the full penalty for all our sins. God raised Jesus from the dead. Jesus ascended into heaven and is our surety at the right of the Father in heaven.

What should we see in the day of adversity? We should see a sovereign God who has already done more good to us in His Son than we could ever imagine. His sovereignty plus our pain now equals a sweet submission to the One we know loves us. Calvary proves it; circumstances don't. What God is looking for from us in the day of adversity is not some valiant effort to show our strength and try to straighten what He has bent. Rather, He wants us to accept what comes through His fatherly hand and be glad in His goodness. When we happily yield to the God of our good days and bad, our joy is out of reach from enemies and all circumstances. He is enough.

11

The Good, the Bad, and the Smugly
(7:15–18)

When Ariel and I were first married (OK, maybe for the first twenty-five years), I would say something and she would look at me with a puzzled face and say, "Are you joking?" Growing up, she was deprived of dry wit, sprinkled with satire, irony, and sarcasm. She now thinks I am hilarious.

There are times when reading Qoheleth that we want to ask, "Are you joking?" He smirks. Qoheleth has a style, we could call it "Qoheleth-isms." His style is an acquired taste. This next section, Ecclesiastes 7:16–29, is filled with Qoheleth-isms. Our tour guide is about to take us on a rough part of the ride, with jolts and jerks, stops and starts. Danger! Possible whiplash ahead!

But there is coherency in his message that revolves around wisdom. Qoheleth has taught us that wisdom is valuable but limited. In this section wisdom's value is seen in that it teaches us to clearly avoid two things: perfectionism and adultery. Wisdom also reminds us of two things: our own sinfulness and the scheming sinfulness of others. Qoheleth is going to teach us these things, and the way he goes about it may tempt us to ask, "Are you joking?" So, hold on.

The Poison of Perfectionism (7:15–18)

> [15] In my vain life I have seen everything. There is a righteous man who perishes in his righteousness, and there is a wicked man who prolongs his life in his evildoing.
>
> [16] Be not overly righteous, and do not make yourself too wise. Why should you destroy yourself?
>
> [17] Be not overly wicked, neither be a fool. Why should you die before your time?
>
> [18] It is good that you should take hold of this, and from that withhold not your hand, for the one who fears God shall come out from both of them.

As noted previously, verse 15 probably provides a transition for both sections. As an introduction to verses 16–18, it sets an important context, namely, the way things ought to be is that the righteous ought to live long and prosperous lives and the wicked should have their lights turned out early.[121] But this short life doesn't always turn out that way. This is a dilemma. Asaph wrestled with the prosperity of the wicked in Psalm 73. Job's friends misapply conventional wisdom to Job, who is righteous and suffers the apparent fate of the wicked. This is indeed one of those bent things in this life.

Qoheleth's counsel at this point sounds strange to those familiar with the Bible's wisdom literature.

Verse 16	Verse 17
Do not be overly righteous	Do not be overly wicked
Do not make yourself too wise	Neither be a fool
Why should you destroy yourself?	Why should you die before your time?

Commentators have made a multitude of suggestions regarding the meaning of these strange sounding words. Some have thought that Solomon is advocating moderation, even in

---

[121] Likewise, Proverbs 10:27 says, "The fear of the LORD prolongs life, but the years of the wicked will be short."

wisdom and righteousness and thus leaving some toleration for some moral sloppiness. The key, however, is in the expression, "overly" righteous and "overly" wise.[122]   Righteousness and wisdom cannot straighten what God has bent, and in the final analysis, attempting to be excessively righteous or overly wise is neither righteous nor wise. The warning is against attempting to do the impossible with the outcome being self-righteousness. Think here of the perfectionist. He or she has an excessive focus on control, preoccupied with the firm conviction that everything in life should be flawless. Perfectionists attempt to secure their desired outcomes by trying to control both people and circumstances. The perfectionist, often, sanctimonious, conceited, and scrupulous, is convinced that his formulas will produce the Christian life, the Christian family, or the Christian business he wants.

The real outcome for the perfectionist is self-ruin. Our wisdom is limited. Our righteousness is limited (7:20). We cannot produce what we want to produce by our own righteousness or wisdom. Excessive righteousness and wisdom will only destroy our ability to enjoy life as the gift of God. Why? Perfectionists are typically tight-laced, unhappy people who excel in being critical and fearful. They are critical of everything or everyone who goes against their own impossible standards and fearful that things won't turn out the way they want.

The Foundation of Fear (7:18)

"Do not be overly wicked" does not mean be a little wicked! Qoheleth says, "Do not be a fool." That is possible! But if he had said, "Do not be wicked," that is impossible (cf. 7:20, 29). The clear result of being overly wicked is dying before one's time. Qoheleth does in fact believe in traditional wisdom; he just knows there are plenty of exceptions. In the counsel not to be overly righteous, he warns us that he is not advocating a life of wickedness. Verse 18 brings both themes together by saying,

---

[122] Similarly, the NASB and the NET both speak of avoiding being "excessively righteous." Neither should one be "overly" (NASB) or "excessively" (NET) wise.

"It is good that you should take hold of this, and from that withhold not your hand, for the one who fears God shall come out from both of them" (7:18). We are to hold on to righteousness and not let go of wisdom. Both are good and necessary. Perhaps 7:19–29 shows us what that partially looks like. The fear of God is the key. To live in the fear of the Lord is to maintain a righteous and wise life that ultimately looks to God and not merely to outcomes. The fear of God is submission to His plans (7:13–14) and gives up trying to control people and circumstances. "If you learn to fear God (which is the important thing), you will come out right in both areas."[123]

What is the lesson being taught here? Avoid errant extremes. Avoid the kind of scrupulous life that reduces righteousness to self-righteousness. If you are a perfectionist, realize that this short life is way too short to waste it seeking perfection from yourself, your spouse, your kids, your church, let alone from life. Live in the fear of the Lord, not the fear of failure. Live in the fear of the Lord, not the fear of not having the right formula.

One day after morning service a man approached me and blurted out,

> I don't get it! I don't get it! Here we are! We try to do everything right as a family. We don't have a TV. We homeschool. We don't eat fast food. We don't let our kids watch movies. We have Bible time every day. We even make sure we all take our vitamins. I look around and I see parents who don't do half of what we do, and they are happy. Their kids love the Lord and them! They even let their kids eat fast food. We are doing everything right; I mean, everything! And we are miserable. We don't get along. There is conflict all the time.

---

[123] Wayne Brindle, "Righteousness and Wickedness in Ecclesiastes 7:15–18," in *Reflecting with Solomon: Selected Studies on the Book of Ecclesiastes*, ed. Roy B. Zuck (Eugene, OR: Wipf & Stock, 2003), 313.

> Why are the ones who don't do it right happy, and we, who are doing it right, are miserable?!

What would Solomon say to this man? He would say,

> Look you uptight, sanctimonious, self-righteous priggish soul! You put too much stock in your formulas! You put too much confidence in your own standards, your own wisdom, and your own righteousness. You cannot control outcomes. Stop trying. Hang on to real wisdom, and biblical righteousness. Fear God. Trust Him. Do what you can. Let go of what you can't. Stop ruining yourself. Stop sucking every ounce of joy out of life. Repent of self-righteousness and quit relying on your own wisdom. Go to Chick-Fil-A or In and Out. Catch a movie, and eat a sandwich on white bread once in a while!

How easy it is for us to forget that it is the righteousness of Jesus Christ which is our only righteousness (1 Cor. 1:30). How hard it is for us to not lean on our own wisdom and understanding (Prov. 3:5–6). Qoheleth warns us to avoid the errant extremes. Trust the Lord and walk in dependence on Him.

12

Don't Be a Wise Guy
(7:15–29)

How easy is it to become self-righteous! "There is a kind who is pure in his own eyes, Yet is not washed from his filthiness" (Prov. 30:12, NASB). How easy it is to think we are really wise! "Do you see a man wise in his own eyes? There is more hope for a fool than for him (26:12). There is no protection, only danger, in self-righteousness and being wise in our own eyes. While it is true that real wisdom is limited in its value, there are two things in this text that wisdom teaches us to avoid: perfectionism (7:15–18) and adultery (7:23–26). Furthermore, there are two things that wisdom demands that we remember: our own sinfulness (7:19–22) and the sinful scheming of others (7:27–29). The very things wisdom compels us to remember are the very reasons why we shouldn't try to be overly righteous or overly wise.

    A. Wisdom avoids perfectionism (7:15–18)

        B. Wisdom remembers one's own sinfulness (7:19–22)

    A. Wisdom avoids adultery (7:23–26)

        B. Wisdom remembers the sinfulness of others (7:27–29)

Know Thyself (7:19–22)

Since we have already covered "wisdom avoids perfectionism," we move on to "wisdom remembers one's own sinfulness."

> [19] Wisdom gives strength to the wise man more than ten rulers who are in a city.
>
> [20] Surely there is not a righteous man on earth who does good and never sins.
>
> [21] Do not take to heart all the things that people say, lest you hear your servant cursing you.
>
> [22] Your heart knows that many times you yourself have cursed others.

Wisdom gives strength, so hold on to wisdom (7:18). Ten rulers in a city may help curb wickedness in the city, but the wise man rules himself and is much stronger than one merely ruled by others. "Power from within is needed, more than advice from without."[124] Qoheleth immediately reminds us, however, that no one is truly righteous. This is why we must not try to be overly righteous: none of us are righteous. Wisdom helps us avoid excessive sinfulness, but it cannot completely remove all sin from our hearts.

Not only should we be realistic with ourselves, but we should be realistic with others. Don't get upset when someone sins against you with their words. You and I have both done it too. We are all sinners who need to learn to deal with people as they are. This is another reason we should not attempt to be overly righteous: it will only lead to holding others to standards that we ourselves fail to meet (Matt. 7:2; Rom. 2:1). This wisdom reminds me of my own sinfulness and my own tendency to sinfully judge others.

A Fate Worse than Death (7:23–26)

> [23] All this I have tested by wisdom. I said, "I will be wise," but it was far from me.
>
> [24] That which has been is far off, and deep, very deep; who can find it out?

---

[124] Eaton, *Ecclesiastes*, 131.

²⁵ I turned my heart to know and to search out and to seek wisdom and the scheme of things, and to know the wickedness of folly and the foolishness that is madness.

²⁶ And I find something more bitter than death: the woman whose heart is snares and nets, and whose hands are fetters. He who pleases God escapes her, but the sinner is taken by her.

Perhaps verse 23 is Qoheleth's confession that he had tried to be "overly wise," and he discovered that the wisdom he was seeking was far from him. Perhaps it was in the mysteries of life that he realized there are far more things beyond his reach than within his grasp. The mysteries remind us of how limited we are (Job 28:12–23; Prov. 30:1–4). Qoheleth turns his sights to wanting to understand the evil of folly and the foolishness of madness. His goal was not to experience it, but to gain wisdom to avoid it. We cannot avoid being sinners, but we can certainly avoid a life given over to evil and folly. Wisdom will help us not to fall into those ditches.

Qoheleth found something. He found something "more bitter than death." What could be more bitter than death for Qoheleth? Hasn't he mourned and complained about death throughout? In his investigation he found something more bitter than that enemy, death, and it was the adulteress woman. The vivid imagery of snares, nets, and chains recalls the adulteress woman in Proverbs 5:3–5; 6:23–35; 7:22–27. She is a hunter. She is more bitter than death because of the pain of conscience and the pain caused to others. Adultery is the height of folly. Sexual sin is a peculiar evil and special kind of folly. For those "looking for love in all the wrong places,"[125] God has a special surprise. Doug Wilson vividly captures it, saying, "Foolish men believe they have found sexual liberty at just the moment when God has seized them by their yearning little idol in order to dash

---

[125] Written by Wanda Mallette, Bob Morrison, and Patti Ryan, and performed by Johnny Lee, "Looking for Love," track 1 on *Looking for Love*, Asylum Records, 1980.

them against the rocks. Their exhilarating sensation of liberty is only temporary—a free fall with death at the end of it."[126]

We must have a heart for God and a heart of wisdom. We must live in the fear of the Lord and He will deliver and spare us. If we have a sensual and seductive heart, God may repay with bitterness worse than death.

In Search of Schemers (7:27–29)

[27] Behold, this is what I found, says the Preacher, while adding one thing to another to find the scheme of things—

[28] which my soul has sought repeatedly, but I have not found. One man among a thousand I found, but a woman among all these I have not found.

[29] See, this alone I found, that God made man upright, but they have sought out many schemes.

Qoheleth admits that he tried to discover the overall scheme of things. He has added one thing to another to try to find out the sum of the whole. It seems that the broader context pushes us back to wisdom in its elusiveness. Wisdom is rare, and its rarity provides another reason why we shouldn't try to be overly wise. The remainder of the text is challenging. A wooden rendering of Ecclesiastes 7:27–29 would be:

"See, this I have found," says Qoheleth

"One to one to find a sum, which I still seek but have not found

One man among a thousand I found/but a woman among all these I did not find a woman.

See this only I have found that God made Man upright,
but they sought many sums/devices/plans."
(*Author's translation*)

---

[126] Wilson, *Joy at the End of the Tether*, 87–88.

What is he looking for in verses 27–28? He is probably looking for a truly wise and truly righteous person. Qoheleth's statistics have been troubling to some. He says he's only able to find one man in a thousand (who is wise) but not one woman. Maybe he is counting himself. Maybe he is thinking of King-Adam. The point is that as he has tried to put things together, connect the dots, and draw some conclusions. His summation has been impossible because he could only find one man and no women in a thousand. Before we get our hackles up, let's remember that Solomon personifies wisdom as a female (Prov. 1:20–33; 8:1–36; 9:1–6). His point may be as simple as the jury is still out on the final tally, but at this juncture in the study, it seems clear that there is not a whole lot of wisdom out there.

Why so pessimistic? Qoheleth discovered that human beings are schemers in sin. God created man upright, but since then, they have sought out many plans or devices. Those plans are not specifically identified as good or evil, but most assuredly they are in contrast with being made upright. As Matthew Poole has said, "[Adam and Eve,] not content with their present state, aimed at higher things, and studied new ways of making themselves wiser and happier than God had made them, and readily hearkened to the suggestions of the devil to that end. And we their sinful and wretched children, who follow after their example, are still prone to forsake the certain rule of God's word, and the true way to happiness, and to seek new methods and inventions of attaining to it."[127]

Conclusion

Trying to be overly wise is short-sighted. It is beyond us. Trying to be overly righteous is short-sighted. It too is beyond us. We need to be secure in the righteousness of Jesus. All my ethical righteousness needs to flow out of the righteousness I have in Jesus. We need to be honest with ourselves and our own weakness and sinfulness.

---

[127] Matthew Poole, *Annotations upon the Holy Bible*, vol. 2 (New York: Robert Carter and Brothers, 1853), 296.

This keeps us humble and dependent on Jesus. We need to remember that when others sin against us, we are ripe for becoming a hypocrite. We need to see the destructive danger of excessive wickedness, especially sexual sin. There is forgiveness, but there are also consequences. We need to be realistic in knowing that we are wired to plan and scheme. We are wired to waste our breath. Such scheming leads us away from wisdom and joy. Be suspicious of yourself. Fear God, and be wise. Wisdom has its limits, but it can help us avoid ruin. It can help us not to waste our breath.

13

It's a Mad, Mad World
(8:1–17)

We live in an upside-down world. As we try to navigate through the world's vertigo, we discover that wisdom is limited. Sometimes wisdom is effective. Sometimes it is ineffective. Exasperation, disorientation, and even spiritual nausea are real in an upside-down world. The burden is real. No matter how much wisdom we have and how much we try to apply it, wisdom often fails to lighten the burden. First, wisdom cannot discover what God is doing, although we know He is doing something. There is so much mystery, too much fog, for us to have clear sight. The future is unclear, though it seems undeniably bleak based on current trajectories. What can we do? Time would fail me if I listed all the occasions my wife and I sat there and read an article or watched a news segment and said, "How much more can we take? How much longer can this crazy world go on like this?" Again, what can we do? When the world around seems like it is one massive multiple car pile-up, what can we do? Qoheleth holds his hand to the side of his mouth and whispers, "Fear God and enjoy life."

Wisdom's Sweetness (8:1)

¹ Who is like the wise?

And who knows the interpretation of a thing?
A man's wisdom makes his face shine,
and the hardness of his face is changed.

Real wisdom, as Qoheleth has already concluded, is rare. "Who is wise? Who knows the interpretation of a matter," brings the reader's mind to rare exceptions like Joseph and Daniel.[128] Both were wise, both possessed gifts of insight to understand a matter. Although wisdom is rare and limited, Qoheleth will not let us leave it aside because of this reality. Rather, he continues to extol wisdom's positive benefits. One of the positive benefits is that it illumines the wise and causes his stern face to beam. Wisdom, in an upside-down world, can bring a bright spot or two. It can also sweeten a rough exterior. Wisdom fears and trusts God. So after watching the latest depressing news story, don't clinch your jaw and let the weight of the world land on your shoulders. Take a breath, lift your eyes to the heavens, and give thanks that there is a God who rules this messed up world. Trust Him and rejoice that He writes the last chapters. "Anxiety, anger, sorrow and frustration can create a hardened facial expression, but the enjoyment of life with wisdom will bring it some relief."[129]

A King's Caution (8:2–9)

> [2] I say: Keep the king's command, because of God's oath to him.
>
> [3] Be not hasty to go from his presence. Do not take your stand in an evil cause, for he does whatever he pleases.
>
> [4] For the word of the king is supreme, and who may say to him, "What are you doing?"
>
> [5] Whoever keeps a command will know no evil thing, and the wise heart will know the proper time and the just way.

---

[128] Daniel lived approximately 400–500 years after Solomon. Joseph, of course, lived centuries before Solomon.

[129] Fredericks, "Ecclesiastes," 186.

⁶ For there is a time and a way for everything, although man's trouble lies heavy on him.

⁷ For he does not know what is to be, for who can tell him how it will be?

⁸ No man has power to retain the spirit, or power over the day of death. There is no discharge from war, nor will wickedness deliver those who are given to it.

⁹ All this I observed while applying my heart to all that is done under the sun, when man had power over man to his hurt.

Qoheleth expounds on effective wisdom with a king in an upside-down world. The context is probably for one who is in the king's court, but the principles certainly apply more broadly. First, wisdom obeys the king (Rom. 13:1–5; 1 Pet. 2:13–17). This obedience is "because of God's oath to him." When Qoheleth speaks of "God's oath," he has in mind an oath someone makes to God. For this reason, the CSB says, "Because of your oath made before God." Likewise, the NET captures it well, saying, "Because you took an oath before God to be loyal to him." A wise man keeps his oath (5:2–6). Wisdom not only obeys the king, but it stays loyal to him. The wise man is not quick to abandon the king and take a stand in an evil cause. Dissent is dangerous. Rebellion is suicidal. Remember, coups have a long history of failure and kings have a long history of making them fatal.

Qoheleth, who knew the power of being king, asserts that the word of the king is supreme. He has little if any human accountability. It is hard for us who live in a democratic republic to imagine authority like this. But "the terror of the king is like the growling of a lion; whoever provokes him to anger forfeits his life" (Prov. 20:2). Therefore, watch your words when in the presence of the one in authority. The bottom line is if you follow the rules, stay loyal, and keep the law, you lessen your chances of getting into hot water or losing your head. But positively, there is a pragmatic reason for being wise in words and obedient in conduct. It is that the wise man picks his battles carefully and knows there are more opportune times for diplomacy with the king. Being an obedient, loyal subject may buy him some goodwill with the king when he must speak up for conscience's sake.

Ecclesiastes 8:6 poses some challenges. It reads, "For there is a time and a way for everything, although man's trouble lies heavy on him." The idea is probably that the wise man will be burdened by many moral concerns. Many issues may be pressing and seem to demand attention, but the wise man in his burden realizes he cannot plant a flag on every hill and be prepared to die there. "Prudence is not necessarily cowardice or compromise."[130] But Qoheleth quickly says that even the most opportune time, wisely chosen, cannot secure a positive outcome. Verse 7 states the ultimate limitation of the wise man: he does not know the future and he certainly cannot control it. We do not know what burdens will be lifted or what matters will see resolution. We do not know if those in authority will ultimately do right, even if we present wise counsel and stand for good causes. We just don't know.

Verse 8 presents four rapid-fire statements. It is very possible that there are only two main statements, each of which is illustrated. The NET takes this approach:

> Just as no one has power over the wind to restrain it,
>   so no one has power over the day of his death.
> Just as no one can be discharged during the battle,
>   so wickedness cannot rescue the wicked. (Eccl. 8:8)

The first statement is probably better understood as "wind," as opposed to the ESV's "spirit."[131] No one has authority over the wind (a common theme in Ecclesiastes). God has control over it, but we don't. Not even the king can control the wind. Just as sure as no one can control the wind, so no one has the power of the day of one's death. God alone has that power; He is in ultimate control of the day we enter this world and the day we leave it.

130 Wilson, *Joy at the End of the Tether*, 93.
131 The Hebrew word for "wind" (*ruach*) can also mean "breath" or "spirit."

The second statement considers the soldier on the battlefield. No matter how dangerous the battle is, the king's word keeps you on the field. Just as sure as you won't be discharged in the middle of a battle, so wickedness will not deliver those given over to it. Wickedness will no more deliver you than the word of the king will deliver the soldier fighting on the battlefield. Fredericks notes, "Although wickedness is perverse, it will not ultimately prevail for those addicted to it."[132]

Qoheleth then concludes his cautionary comments: "All this I observed while applying my heart to all that is done under the sun, when man had power over man to his hurt" (8:9). Qoheleth has told us how to maintain good relations with the king. He has urged obedience and loyalty. He has counseled patience, even in burdensome matters. He has warned us that we do not know how things will turn out no matter how wise we are. And now he wraps it up and says that even with such wise behavior and submission to authority, that authority can still be abused and people can be hurt. Life under the sun in this death row cell is life that is subject to both death and injustice. Not even the wise can avert the abuse of power.

Funerals Full of Lies (8:10–13)

> [10] Then I saw the wicked buried. They used to go in and out of the holy place and were praised in the city where they had done such things. This also is vanity.
>
> [11] Because the sentence against an evil deed is not executed speedily, the heart of the children of man is fully set to do evil.
>
> [12] Though a sinner does evil a hundred times and prolongs his life, yet I know that it will be well with those who fear God, because they fear before him.
>
> [13] But it will not be well with the wicked, neither will he prolong his days like a shadow, because he does not fear before God.

---

[132] Fredericks, "Ecclesiastes," 194.

Are the wicked praised or forgotten? The ESV says they are praised (8:10). The NASB says they are forgotten. "Forgotten" may be the better reading (cf. 2:16), but "praise" makes better sense even though it is a variant.[133] With verse 9 as the backdrop, the wicked are those who hurt others, then they die and are buried. They have extravagant funerals, with all the pomp and circumstance. They were wicked, and they were religious. When they die and have their funeral, they are praised. What an injustice. What motivation is there to avoid evil and pursue righteousness when the wicked are spoken so highly of at their funeral, with only their temple attendance and "good deeds" remembered?

Another incentive to do evil is found in verse 11 (i.e., no consequence for bad behavior). When there are no consequences to bad behavior. When a just sentence is not carried out against a criminal, the message is that you can get away with whatever crime you choose to commit. This was true in ancient times, and it is true today—as district attorneys in certain states send a message when they get softer and softer on crime and make policies that do not send criminals to jail, such as no cash bail. That message is there are no consequences to bad behavior. The righteous know that the swift punishment of evildoers deters wickedness in a society. When justice is not swift, it only fuels more and more evil.

The fool may believe that crime really pays. He may conclude that there are no consequences to hurting others. But the wise man knows that even if a sinner commits a hundred crimes, doesn't pay for them, and lives a long life, it will still go better for God-fearing people. The fool walks by sight. The wise man walks by faith. Faith says true shalom rests on those who fear the Lord and payday someday for the rest. Fearing the Lord has

---

[133] Eaton (*Ecclesiastes*, 139) provides helpful commentary for deciding between these two possible readings. He writes that changing forgotten to praised "involves a minute emendation of *wĕyištakkĕḥu* ('they were forgotten') to *wĕyištabbĕḥu* ('they were praised'), which is almost certainly correct. The Hebrew letters *beth* and *kaph* are similar; there is support in the ancient versions and in some Hebrew manuscripts. The verse is dealing with an injustice (*they were praised*), not a rightful retribution (*they were forgotten*)."

true reward, but not fearing Him has destructive consequences. The problem with the fool is that he lives life based on how things appear. The wise man knows that things are not as they appear to be. The lengthening of days for the wicked is an illusion because in the end, just like everyone else, his life is a vapor. He lives his vapor without fearing God and when he breathes his last, the full terror of such a godless life will land on him with the weight of eternity.

The Cinnamon Roll Center (8:14–17)

¹⁴ There is a vanity that takes place on earth, that there are righteous people to whom it happens according to the deeds of the wicked, and there are wicked people to whom it happens according to the deeds of the righteous. I said that this also is vanity.

¹⁵ And I commend joy, for man has nothing better under the sun but to eat and drink and be joyful, for this will go with him in his toil through the days of his life that God has given him under the sun.

¹⁶ When I applied my heart to know wisdom, and to see the business that is done on earth, how neither day nor night do one's eyes see sleep,

¹⁷ then I saw all the work of God, that man cannot find out the work that is done under the sun. However much man may toil in seeking, he will not find it out. Even though a wise man claims to know, he cannot find it out.

We have a wonderful woman in our church who wages war against my battle with the beltline. She makes cinnamon rolls to die for. My wife and I love them. "Well, we better eat the rest of them so that they are no longer around," is the logic. Now anyone who is a cinnamon roll connoisseur knows it is the center of the cinnamon roll that is the best part. With the center being the sweet spot, we revisit a well-known theme in Ecclesiastes that we can rightly call "the cinnamon roll center."

As vapor appears in verse 14, it has a painful implication. The mist of *hebel* brings forth an absurdity in this life. There are righteous people, and they suffer like the wicked should, and there are wicked people who are apparently rewarded like the righteous should be. The *hebel* of life introduces all kinds of mysteries. One of them is that the way things ought to be is not the way things are. Shalom is vandalized. The scales of justice are knocked over. This is Psalm 73. It is painful. But it is still a vapor. The vandalism of shalom does not last forever; it is a mere breath. What shall we do in such a world? Qoheleth says, "I commend joy!" In an upside-down, mad, mad world, Qoheleth says, "Go for the center of the cinnamon roll!"

The joy he praises is the affection of contentment and satisfaction that we have deep in our souls. He commends joy because "he values it as the most durable and valuable result of human endeavors."[134] We need to stop for a moment. We value honesty. We value integrity. We value hard work. But do we value joy? Is joy a value to us? Is it a value worth pursuing? Qoheleth believed it to be so. He tells us in this death row existence to eat, drink, and be joyful; we must embrace and enjoy the blessings of this life. This is exactly how you navigate life in an upside-down world.

As you enjoy the center of the cinnamon roll, don't forget God's work is still incomprehensible. So when we are burdened with a world gone mad, when troubles assail us, when nothing seems to make sense, what do we need to know? We don't need to know what God is doing to have joy. In a world gone crazy, I need to stick with the basics: life is a vapor, life is a mystery, God is in charge, fear him, trust him, and always eat the center of the cinnamon roll.

---

[134] Farmer, *Proverbs and Ecclesiastes*, 183.

14

How to Live Before You Die
(9:1–10)

God created the world, and He made it good (Gen. 1:31).
To be sure, sin has vandalized the beauty of creation and
spoiled God's good gifts. To be sure, the devil has perverted both
this life and the things of earth, so that we worship what we ought
to enjoy and destroy it in the process. These are painful truths.
The church has often responded to the realities of this fallen
world with a disdain for it. For instance, Isaac Watts writes, in
the hymn, "How Vain Are All the Things Here Below,"

> How vain are all things here below;
> How false, and yet how fair!
> Each pleasure has its poison too,
> And every sweet a snare.[135]

However, Qoheleth says, "So I commend pleasure" (Eccl.
8:15). Which is it? Is everything here below, every pleasure,
every sweet thing, simply a poison and a snare? Or is there joy
in the things here below? Watts was not completely wrong, but
the tendency we have toward asceticism in the Christian life is

---

[135] Quoted by Joe Rigney, *The Things of Earth: Treasuring God by Enjoying His Gifts*
(Wheaton, IL: Crossway, 2015), 23. The introduction to this chapter is strongly influ-
enced by Joe's insights, pages, 22–25.

a common one. The message of the Bible is that enjoying God's good gifts glorifies God. Enjoying, not worshiping, the things of earth, helps us to worship God. David Gibson tells us, "God takes pleasure in your pleasure. He's given it to you."[136] The joy that God provides in the mist, the joys that are vapors, are still gifts. They can become a snare if we allow them to move us away from our anchor, but they are not snares and poison in themselves. The good gifts only become a snare when we try to get more out of them than God has designed. The good gifts only become poison when we bestow godhood on them and then worship and serve them. Then they sting us with their venom in the end. Gifts are gifts, not gods. Qoheleth says, "Keep that in perspective, then take a full swing at enjoyment!"

This section of Ecclesiastes is Ecclesiastes in a nutshell. It gives us a perspective on life, death, God, and joy. Qoheleth leads us through this part of the journey and shows us something worth living for, namely, how to put death to shame by really living before you die.

The Mystery of Providence (9:1–3)

> [1] But all this I laid to heart, examining it all, how the righteous and the wise and their deeds are in the hand of God. Whether it is love or hate, man does not know; both are before him.
>
> [2] It is the same for all, since the same event happens to the righteous and the wicked, to the good and the evil, to the clean and the unclean, to him who sacrifices and him who does not sacrifice. As the good one is, so is the sinner, and he who swears is as he who shuns an oath.
>
> [3] This is an evil in all that is done under the sun, that the same event happens to all. Also, the hearts of the children of man are full of evil, and madness is in their hearts while they live, and after that they go to the dead.

---

[136] Gibson, *Living Life Backwards*, 112.

Qoheleth has affirmed God's sovereignty (3:1–8; 7:15). He has also told us that things do not always work out with the righteous and the wicked, as we might expect. Now, in 9:1 he explicitly tells us that he has taken this theological problem to heart. He has tried to explain it, and yet, in the end, all he can say is the deeds of the righteous and the deeds of the wicked are in the hand of God. The theological tension is clear enough, but then he adds an interesting expression. He writes, "Man does not know whether it will be love or hatred; both are before him." The righteous and the wise have no guarantees that their deeds will produce a smiling providence. Although they are in the sovereign hand of God, sovereignty is not predictable. Either "love" or "hatred" may await. Both are possibilities. Graham Ogden notes, "We assume that these two terms refer to either a bright or gloomy future, 'love' speaking of God's graciousness, and 'hate' representing a future that is to be feared."[137] The key is not simply that both are possibilities, but that "anything awaits them."

We may ask, "Who are the friends of God?" You cannot tell God's friends by who is blessed and who is not. "Who is loved by God?" You cannot tell by God's treatment of them in this life. The great Mark Twain reportedly said, "God would have more friends if he treated the ones he had a little better."[138] Tevye from *Fiddler on the Roof* complained, "I know, I know. We are your chosen people. But, once in a while, can't you choose someone else?" Although we may smile at Twain's and Tevye's candidness, Qoheleth has taught us that prosperity is not always a blessing (6:1–6) and adversity is not always evil (7:1–15). We should be catching on now that there is no formula that interprets life or God's actions. There is no rubric that explains what events in life constitute either God's love and God's hate or God's blessing and God's judgment.

---

[137] Ogden, *Qoheleth*, 145.

[138] Similarly, Teresa of Avila, a medieval catholic nun and mystic, supposedly responded to perceived mistreatment from Jesus saying, "If this is how you treat your friends, no wonder you have so few of them."

Everyone Dies (9:2–3)

Old news from Qoheleth's news desk: you are going to die no matter how you live. Gibson remarks, "If you expect good people to get a fair deal from the grim reaper, then you have a very bitter pill to swallow. This is the way the world is to all."[139] The same event—death —happens to the good, the bad, the religious, the irreligious, the one who makes oaths and is faithful to his vows, and the one who breaks or shuns vows. Everyone dies. Perhaps Qoheleth would have laughed at a news article out of New Orleans in 2004. It read, "Vitamin E actually increases the risk of dying, according to new findings." Increase the risk the dying? Breathing increases the risk of dying. The stats so far are consistent: one out of one die.

No matter how often Qoheleth reminds us of this sobering truth, it is easy to see he is never comfortable with it. It is an evil done under the sun. The same rotten event happens to all. And even knowing that, man still lives a life full of evil. Man is barely above the beasts (3:18), and his passions make him a spiritually insane being who does not function according to truth, logic, or reality. Rather he operates on the simple beastly principle of wanting what he wants. This pattern is consistent throughout his life, but it comes to a screeching halt when his heart stops and he fills his lungs for the last time. He then goes to the dead.

A Living Dog and a Dead Lion (9:4–6)

> [4] But he who is joined with all the living has hope, for a living dog is better than a dead lion.
>
> [5] For the living know that they will die, but the dead know nothing, and they have no more reward, for the memory of them is forgotten.
>
> [6] Their love and their hate and their envy have already perished, and forever they have no more share in all that is done under the sun.

---

[139] Gibson, *Living Life Backwards*, 108.

By now we should be acquainted with Qoheleth's unconventional, even startling language. This passage is not a statement inferring that there is no hope in the life to come. Rather it is a straightforward comment made from this side of the grave. Life is to be preferred over death. Hope in this life is the hope of enjoying God's good gifts before time and opportunity are no more.

"Surely a live dog is better than a dead lion." No Israelite in their right mind would have domesticated a dog and taught it to fetch the *Jerusalem Times*. Dogs were held in contempt. But the lion, now there's a beast to be admired. Strong, fierce, regal, and feared! Qoheleth is so committed to breathing in this world that he says a live dog is better than a dead lion. But, "the living know they will die." The reason it is better to be a live dog is because the living has time to reckon with the reality of death. The dead have lost that opportunity; it is too late. To live in light of one's impending death affords us the opportunity to be prepared to meet God, and it also empowers us to embrace this life as a gift to enjoy. Those who know they are going to die are best equipped to enjoy this fleeting life. Death brings an end to those opportunities.

"The dead know nothing, and they have no more reward, for the memory of them is forgotten" (9:5). Qoheleth does not have a fully developed view of the life to come, but he is not talking about heaven. He is talking about the grave from the above-ground perspective. Once we breathe our last, there is no more ability to enjoy the things of this life. And then that enemy, death, causes our memory to fade. Verse 6 underscores this vividly. When someone dies there is no longer an occasion to converse with them, to hug them, to laugh about our favorite memories, or make new memories. Death is an enemy that robs us of life. Herman Bavinck captures the sentiment, "Death breaks the varied and wonderful bonds of life relations in this world.

In comparison with life on this side of the grave, death results in non-being, the disturbing negation of the rich and joyful experience on earth."[140]

Qoheleth never romanticizes death. Death is not freedom. Death is not a friend. Death is not an escape from trouble. Death is a vile enemy. He is pained by the fact that what makes this life a breath is that it is over so quickly. There is only one way it ends, and that is death. It is death that puts the period at the end of life, and it always jots it down way too soon. How many have retired with a nice nest egg, only to die a short time afterwards? Death is no respecter of our expectations.

Now the real question at the end of this section is this: how shall we live knowing we are going to die? This is such an important question. Qoheleth, for his part, is determined to not allow death to rob him of God's gifts. He will not be swindled out of joy. He wants us to learn this too. Qoheleth is all about kicking death in the teeth by really living while we live. Qoheleth shows us how to defang death by embracing the gift with all its joys.

How to Live Before You Die (9:7–10)

> [7] Go, eat your bread with joy, and drink your wine with a merry heart, for God has already approved what you do.
>
> [8] Let your garments be always white. Let not oil be lacking on your head.
>
> [9] Enjoy life with the wife whom you love, all the days of your vain life that he has given you under the sun, because that is your portion in life and in your toil at which you toil under the sun.
>
> [10] Whatever your hand finds to do, do it with your might, for there is no work or thought or knowledge or wisdom in Sheol, to which you are going.

---

[140] Herman Bavinck, *Holy Spirit, Church, and New Creation*, vol 4 of *Reformed Dogmatics*, ed. John Bolt, trans. Jon Vriend (Grand Rapids: Baker Academic, 2008), 607.

The following section is not some resignation to the meaninglessness of life with the only path being to anesthetize oneself with pleasure. This is a call to full-orbed sanctification. God's will for your life is to enjoy this life. God commands you to enjoy this life, in the *hebel*, in the mystery, in the sadness, and even in the pain. Qoheleth is going to lay down some seriously spiritual advice here. So buckle up and prepare to receive the profound spiritual counsel from the sage of sages.

Enjoy Your Food (9:7)

"Go, eat your bread with joy" (9:7). "Hey, wait a minute, I thought you said Qoheleth was going to lay down some super spiritual stuff to help me live before I die. 'Enjoy my food?' How is that spiritual?" I am so glad you asked! We have such a narrow, pietistic view of spirituality. We have an ethereal view of the Christian life that says it must be mystical to be spiritual. Nonsense! "When men understand the futility of earthly existence, and they understand it in the way Solomon presents it to us, they are then equipped to enjoy their bread perhaps for the first time."[141]

Food is the gift of God, and good tasting food is the good gift of God. God takes delight when we enjoy His gifts. So kick death in the teeth by marinating the rib eyes, lighting up the barbeque, and baking the potatoes. Spiritually use butter and sour cream. Don't forget a salad for conscience's sake and enjoy it all to the glory of God. As the food delights the taste buds, give thanks to the One who provided it. Don't over-eat and abuse God's gifts but enjoy the food that He has given (1 Tim. 4:4–5).

The next imperative may cause some Baptist anxieties or downright panic attacks. Ecclesiastes 9:7 continues, "Drink your wine with a cheerful heart." Wine in the Bible is not seen from the prohibitionist's perspective but rather as a gift from God (Ps. 104:14–15). Wine's connection with God's blessings and with

---

[141] Wilson, *Joy at the End of the Tether*, 101.

celebration is unmistakable.[142] Qoheleth is not advocating abusing God's gifts but using them for His glory through our enjoyment.[143]

Ecclesiastes 9:7 then ends with a statement of liberation: "For God has already approved what you do." The NASB puts it this way: "For God has already approved your works." Our works are in the hands of God (9:1). If we live by the standard formulas of spiritual success and the fallible interpretations of providence, then we will never know whether we are accepted by God (9:1). We will never know if our good works are good enough. We will never know how our failures factor in. Did my bad deed cause this bad thing to happen? But if we live by divine revelation, knowing that God has accepted us and our works, then we are not on the performance track, trying to eke out some favor from the Most High. Rather we are liberated to be on the "already accepted" track, and we have the capacity to enjoy life as God's good gift. Assurance of acceptance with God empowers us to enjoy God and His gifts without second-guessing ourselves at every turn.

Be a Joyful Person (9:8)

"Let your garments be always white. Let not oil be lacking on your head" (9:8). This prescription for really living before you die is to be a joyful person! The garb described is the opposite of sackcloth and ashes, which is the apparel of grief. This is celebratory. Qoheleth is not saying, "Wear cool clothes and get an expensive haircut." But he is saying, "Don't walk around like the sky is falling. Don't be a miserable old crank!" Maybe the sky is falling, but that too is a vapor, so don't let it rob you of your vapor. "The charge of melancholy is a libel upon religion."[144]

---

[142] See Kenneth Gentry, *God Gave Wine* (Lincoln, CA: Oakdown, 2001).

[143] The Bible is clearly against the abuse of alcohol, which is the sin of drunkenness (Eph. 5:18). As Christians, we must make sure that we do not use our liberties in a way that wounds the consciences of others (Rom. 14:1–23).

[144] Bridges, *Ecclesiastes*, 219.

Let me say something about being a miserable person. If you are a joyless, miserable person, no one will miss you when you die. If you are a person who enjoys life as God's gift, you spread that joy. You will be profoundly missed when you die. Here is the obituary of seventy-nine-year-old Dolores Aguilar that was recorded in the Vallejo California Times Herald (August 16–17, 2008). It was submitted by one of her daughters.

> Dolores Aguilar, born August 7, 1929, died, August 22, 2008. Dolores Aguilar, born in 1929 in New Mexico, left us on August 7, 2008. She will be met in the afterlife by her husband, Raymond, her son, Paul Jr., and daughter, Ruby....

> Dolores had no hobbies, made no contribution to society, and rarely shared a kind word or deed in her life. I speak for the majority of her family when I say her presence will not be missed by many, very few tears will be shed and there will be no lamenting over her passing.

> Her family will remember Dolores and amongst ourselves we will remember her in our own way, which were mostly sad and troubling times throughout the years. We may have some fond memories of her and perhaps we will think of those times too. But I truly believe at the end of the day ALL of us will really only miss what we never had, a good and kind mother, grandmother and great-grandmother. I hope she is finally at peace with herself.

> As for the rest of us left behind, I hope this is the beginning of a time of healing and learning to be a family again. There will be no service, no prayers and no closure for the family she spent a lifetime tearing apart. We cannot come together in the end to see to it that her grandchildren and great-grandchildren can say their goodbyes.

So I say here for all of us, GOOD BYE, MOM.[145]

How different is this following tribute to a dear Christian friend who died in 2014:

> Diny was my friend, my mentor, my sister in Christ, my counselor, and my co-worker. I have never met anyone so full of life and so genuine. She knew firsthand that life was hard, but she knew even more that God was good. Her passion for Christ overflowed.... I will always think of her when I listen to the song "I Can Only Imagine...." Diny, I can't wait to see you again in Heaven, your final destination! Unlike you, we are all still just imagining.[146]

Don't live in a way that when you die, people are relieved. Live in such a way that you are missed when you are gone. Be a joyful person, full of life in Jesus. Then when you are with Jesus our family and friends will miss your presence and joy.

Enjoy Your Spouse (9:9)

"Enjoy life with the wife whom you love, all the days of your vain life that he has given you under the sun, because that is your portion in life and in your toil at which you toil under the sun" (9:9). This is one of those verses that strongly demonstrate that *hebel* should not be translated "vain," or "futile," but "vaporous," or "fleeting." The third prescription for living before you die is to enjoy your spouse. Qoheleth shows us that marriage is a vital ingredient in defying death's pall. Marriage is a gift from God. It is joining together one man and one woman in love, for life. It is significant that in the passage Qoheleth adds the words "whom you love."

---

[145] Jim Elliff, "When Nobody Misses You," https://bulletininserts.org/when-nobody-misses-you/, capitalization original.

[146] This was taken from a book of remembrances for Diane Gamble, a long-time member of our congregation who died unexpectedly in 2014. She is still greatly missed.

"The point is that a man should marry a woman he loves, not say, one who only brings a hefty dowry or family connections."[147]

Romance, sexual intimacy, and companionship in marriage are supposed to be among the most exquisite delights in this short, blip-on-the-screen life. When Qoheleth says, "All the days of your fleeting life," he is telling us that marriage brings a sweetness to this short life. Marriage is an elixir in our death row cell under the sun. It is part of our portion, our reward, in the midst of toil. Since that is God's design, there ought to be a sanctified indulgence in the joys of marriage. As Solomon says, in another place, "Let your fountain be blessed and rejoice in the wife of your youth. As a loving hind and a graceful doe, let her breasts satisfy you at all times.

Be exhilarated always with her love" (Prov. 5:18–19). The word "exhilarated" is the word for "intoxicated." This is the only intoxication advocated or allowed in the Bible!

For some, God has not given this marvelous gift. Some remain single their whole lives. If that is you, you need to understand, marriage is not what completes you. It is Jesus Christ who completes you. If God withholds this gift from you, seek contentment in Him and look to the other gifts He has given you to enjoy.

For those of us who enjoy the gift, remember, God will one day take it from us. For some, He already has. When that day comes and your spouse enters the Lord's presence, there will assuredly be sadness and sorrow. The happier the marriage, the deeper the sadness. But make sure you are thankful that you enjoyed the gift while you had it. I have always been struck by the words of Sarah Edwards, wife of Jonathan Edwards, written to her daughter Esther, upon hearing the news of her Jonathan's death,

---

[147] Michael V. Fox, *A Time to Tear Down and a Time to Build Up: A Rereading of Ecclesiastes* (Grand Rapids: Eerdmans, 1999), 294.

My Very Dear Child,

What shall I say? A holy and good God has covered us with a dark cloud. O that we may kiss the rod, and lay our hands on our mouths! The Lord has done it. He has made me adore his goodness, that we had him so long. But my God lives; and he has my heart. O what a legacy my husband, and your father, has left us! We are all given to God; and there I am, and love to be.

Your ever affectionate mother,

Sarah Edwards.[148]

For however long you had each other, it was a gift of God.

For those who have the gift, but do not enjoy it, repent. One responds, "Too much water under the bridge." Nonsense. God is a God of restoration. He makes up for the years the locusts have eaten (Joel 2:25). "Well, I don't like my gift. I wish I had a different one." Repent. That husband or that wife is the one God gave you. Don't ruin the gift by wishing it was a different year or model. Grumbling and complaining are the echoes of a discontent heart. Maybe God has some serious work to do on you or on your gift. He most certainly does. So pray together. Pray for each other. Read the Word together. God shall hold us accountable if we made our spouse miserable.

Be an Earnest Person (9:10)

"Whatever your hand finds to do, do it with your might, for there is no work or thought or knowledge or wisdom in Sheol, to which you are going" (Eccl. 9:10). Qoheleth concludes his prescriptions with the command to have a positive, robust, hearty, approach to life and work. There is nothing half-hearted about Qoheleth. Be an earnest, diligent person, who pours yourself into whatever is before you, whether that is your work, your marriage, your worship, or your play. Half-heartedness in this life sucks the joy

---

[148] George Marsden, *Jonathan Edwards: A Life* (New Haven, CT: Yale University Press, 2003), 495.

out of it. Earnestness in life is what helps us to enjoy it. Now don't let the refrain about death unsettle you. Solomon brings it up, not to scare us, but to motivate us. Who wants to live an insipid, lethargic existence and then die? Jonathan Edwards's sixth resolution hits the nail on the head: "Resolved, to live with all my might, while I do live."[149]

Conclusion

A distorted view of worldliness may sap the pleasures out of the very life that God has commanded us to enjoy. We may end up treating the things of earth with disdain rather than receiving them as temporary but good gifts. When we enjoy God's gifts, as gifts, we do not worship them. When we worship them, we are guilty of idolatry. When we enjoy them as God's gifts, God is glorified. We are commanded to enjoy our food, be a joyful person, enjoy our spouse, and be an earnest person. To live like this is to put death to shame.

God's gifts to us in this life are a precursor to a new heaven and a new earth, where we will enjoy all of God's gifts and blessings without the specter of death peering over our shoulders and without the pain the *hebel* brings. These gifts, and more, will be better and brighter, and they will be ours if Jesus Christ is ours. If Jesus Christ, God's greatest gift, is ours by faith, then all lesser gifts in this life "will grow strangely *bright* in the light of his glory and grace."[150] Then in the life to come, all of His greatest gifts will be enjoyed with no more tears, no more pain, and no more death.

---

[149] Jonathan Edwards, "Early Religious Productions. Miscellanies. Notes on Scriptures. Commencement on his preaching. Resolutions" in *The Works of Jonathan Edwards* (Edinburgh: Banner of Truth Trust, 1990), 1.3: xx.

[150] Rigney, *Strangely Bright*, 110, italics original.

When on the day, the great I Am,
The faithful and the true,
The Lamb who was for sinner's slain,
Is making all things new.
Behold our God shall live with us,
And be our steadfast Light,
And we shall e'er his people be,
All glory be to Christ.[151]

[151] Written by Dustin Kensrue and arranged by Kings Kaleidoscope, "All Glory Be to Christ," track 5 on *Joy Has Dawned*, Dead Bird Theology and It's All About Jesus Music, 2012.

15

Expect the Unexpected
(9:11–18)

Many of us were raised to work hard. Hard-working parents modeled that ethic for us and instructed us to work hard. If the leaves were not raked properly, we would go back and do it again until it was done right. Any job worth doing is worth doing well. This is conventional wisdom, and it is common sense. Some were taught they could do anything if they put their mind to it. They could achieve their dreams if they just worked hard enough. The call to hard work, to make hay while the sun shines, to be zealous and intentional, is not merely a good suggestion. It is a command that Qoheleth gave: "Whatever your hand finds to do, do it with your might, for there is no work or thought or knowledge or wisdom in Sheol, to which you are going" (Eccl. 9:10).

On the flipside, the Bible condemns laziness and upbraids the sluggard. The lazy man should have no expectations of a good return on his laziness. We might be tempted to think that if we follow the instruction in 9:10, then things will go well. We have biblical warrant to think that hard work pays off.[152]

---

[152] Such biblical warrant for thinking that hard work pays off is found in Proverbs 22:14a: "The work of a man's hand comes back to him." Yet more comes from Proverbs 22:29: "Do you see a man skillful in his work? He will stand before kings; he will not stand before obscure men."

So maybe if we take Qoheleth as the ancient version of *Poor Richard's Almanac*, then we will have success in life. But Qoheleth refuses to let us live by such simple formulas. The one who lives by simple formulas will have expectations that will often go unmet. The general principles of life are filled with exceptions. Qoheleth now takes to bursting our little formula bubbles.

Time and Chance (9:11–12)

> [11] Again I saw that under the sun the race is not to the swift, nor the battle to the strong, nor bread to the wise, nor riches to the intelligent, nor favor to those with knowledge, but time and chance happen to them all.

> [12] For man does not know his time. Like fish that are taken in an evil net, and like birds that are caught in a snare, so the children of man are snared at an evil time, when it suddenly falls upon them.

Qoheleth is the inspired observer. He is our tour guide. He is our provocateur. He makes five observations about this earthly life under the sun. These observations are about some reasonable expectations in life. But as we will see, just because an expectation is reasonable does not guarantee the desired outcome.

"The race is not to the swift." In a race the fastest runner should win. But sometimes he doesn't win. Sometimes the slower runner comes out of nowhere and passes the faster runner as he thinks he has it made. Second place is the first loser. Asahel overtook Abner since he was the swifter runner. But then he died by the end of Abner's spear (2 Sam. 2:22–23). In that case, faster was fatal.

"The battle is not to the warriors." The well-trained, courageous soldier should be victorious. But often they aren't. The apparent random arrow or bullet, or even friendly fire, takes out the trained warrior.

"Neither is bread to the wise." Wisdom should secure the basics of life, but often it doesn't. Wise people plan. They plan for security, but sometimes they end up begging for their bread.

"Nor wealth to the discerning." The discerning clearly should be able to accumulate wealth. But sometimes their plans fail. The shrewd and insightful should make a profit. They are the ones who know when to buy and when to sell. But sometimes they are the ones to jump out of a window when their wealth has flown away.

"Nor favor to men of ability." Talent and skill should win favor. Often, they do, but many times they don't. The competent and the able are overlooked and ignored. Who is recognized? The one who was more skilled at stealing ideas than honing a skill.

All these examples have certain expectations of success. Skill, effort, diligence, and hard work should all be rewarded. Training and talent should pay off. But Qoheleth says there are no guarantees. The exceptions make us question the rule. The standard of fairness and meritocracy should secure success. But it doesn't always work that way. All these things—speed, skill, wealth, wisdom, and talent—are gifts and blessings from God. But there are other factors to consider. Yes, the sovereignty of God is unpredictable. But here Qoheleth is going to take us down to ground level. There are certain expectations in life based on the way things ought to be, but then those expectations are unmet because of a head-on collision with the unexpected. The unexpected can change everything.

"For time and chance overtake them all." Time overtakes us. Time is in the sovereign hand of God; it is under His control. Expectations may be thwarted simply because in God's time they were not ordained to succeed. "There is no wisdom and no understanding and no counsel against the LORD" (Prov. 21:30). No matter how fast, how strong, how wise, how wealthy, how healthy, or how talented we may be, our times are in God's hands. We cannot trust even the most reasonable expectations in this life.

When I was entering my final year of college, Ariel and I were just married. We were poor. We had no money for seminary, let alone for a costly move from Southern California to Portland, Oregon. But then my hard work paid off. I worked for a mobile car detailer making $60 a day. We were going to move from Santa Ana to Palm Springs for my last semester to live in Ariel's grandparents' vacant home. My boss was elated. He wanted me to start a branch of his detailing business in Palm Springs. He would give me a vehicle, business cards, a pager, and $400 per week for three days of work per week. I could not believe it! I would almost be a millionaire! We could save money. We could get up to Portland for seminary. If I could get some clients in some of the business parks, then the word would spread, the business would grow, and I would be set. My last six months in college would be a booming financial success and set us on solid ground for our move.

Then the unexpected clashed with what looked like God's answer to our prayers. There was a change in corporate auto insurance policies. I would now have to use my own car. A small setback! But the big setback was the heat. Palm Springs was much hotter than the area where I had been washing cars. There was no shade! I put the water on, and it would evaporate before I could wipe it down. Water spots! I tried everything. The only "clients" I had were those who parked in shady spots and were at work by 7:00 a.m. Later than that, the cars got too hot. What seemed like a blessing, an answer to prayer, a reward for my hard work, turned into a heartache as the unexpected squashed my reasonable expectations. God had other plans and other ways to meet our needs, but I didn't know that. I only knew what looked like an answer to prayer was dashed to pieces because of unexpected legislation and the unanticipated effects of the Palm Springs heat.

"Chance overtakes them all." Chance is not what we think it is. We often assume chance is some kind of force that cannot be foreseen or controlled. In God's universe, the scientists' "chance" does not exist. For an Israelite, chance does not mean

---

[153] Eaton, *Ecclesiastes*, 70.

that something is random. "On the lips of an Israelite 'chance' means what is unexpected, not what is random."[153] "Chance is the unexpected event which may throw the most accomplished off course, despite the most thoroughly prepared schemes."[154] Qoheleth is not saying that time and "chance or luck" overtake us. He is simply saying that unexpected events overtake us. Unexpected events turn our lives upside down in a flash.

"Man does not know his time." God is making all things beautiful in His time, but time overtakes us all. The unpredictable happens just like a fish that swims into a net, or a bird trapped by a snare. We do not know what awaits us. Physically fit people die of heart attacks. Marriages made in heaven end in divorce. A career that is on the fast track to success is derailed because of cancer. An enduring friendship dies because of a misunderstanding. A bright future in sports never transpires because of a seemingly insignificant injury. A ministry never grows, never matures, despite gifts and sincerity. There are no guarantees in this life. Everything is in the mysterious hand of providence. The hourglass empties faster than we thought it would or should. The unexpected falls on us like a piano from the sky. This is life under the sun.

The Forgotten Man (9:13–18)

> [13] I have also seen this example of wisdom under the sun, and it seemed great to me.
>
> [14] There was a little city with few men in it, and a great king came against it and besieged it, building great siegeworks against it.

---

[154] Eaton, *Ecclesiastes*, 130. Likewise, R.C. Sproul wrote, "Chance is not an entity. It is not a thing that has power to affect other things. It is no thing. To be more precise, it is *nothing*. Nothing cannot do something. Nothing is not. It has no 'isness.' Chance has no isness. I was technically incorrect even to say that chance is nothing. Better to say that chance is not. What are the chances that chance can do anything? Not a chance." R.C. Sproul, *Not a Chance: The Myth of Chance in Modern Science and Cosmology* (Grands Rapids: Baker Books, 1994), 6.

¹⁵ But there was found in it a poor, wise man, and he by his wisdom delivered the city. Yet no one remembered that poor man.

¹⁶ But I say that wisdom is better than might, though the poor man's wisdom is despised and his words are not heard.

¹⁷ The words of the wise heard in quiet are better than the shouting of a ruler among fools.

¹⁸ Wisdom is better than weapons of war, but one sinner destroys much good.

Qoheleth now tells us something that he observed that impressed him. There are people in my life that are not easily impressed. It seems to me that Qoheleth was one of those guys, so when he says he was impressed, we should pay close attention. He tells us of this small city. The story has all the marks of a great story, a classic story—*Magnificent Seven* stuff! There's a small town and a bad king with bad intentions, seeking to take advantage of the townsfolk and destroy the little town. A hero arises. The hero is a poor but wise man. He is a commoner. He delivers the city. We are not told how, but you can imagine, he outsmarts the evil king (or cattle baron) and saves the town through impressive wisdom (or good fast marksmanship).

What awaits this hero? A parade? The key to the city? A building named after him? Wealth? A town marshal position? None of this happens. His reward is to be forgotten. The deliverer slips into obscurity. The problem is ingratitude. This is what people are like. But that doesn't soften the frustration or the anger. There is something that raises our ire in this story. The hero stands in the gap for the good of the people, and the people, once past the crisis, have no use for the hero, and he is unceremoniously forgotten. Gratitude and honor are reasonable expectations. Neither come to fruition. Once deliverance had come, everything went back to business as usual. There is nothing more frustrating than ingratitude, being taken for granted, and having mercy and sacrifice treated as if it were an obligation or an entitlement.

The first conclusion is *not* "don't worry about wisdom, what good is it anyways?" The conclusion is *not* "stop caring about injustice." The conclusion is *not*, "Forget trying to help people. Rescue a dog instead. They are more grateful." Are these conclusions a temptation? Of course. But the right conclusion is to remember that "wisdom is better than strength." The parable of the poor wise man shows this. Even though his wisdom was forgotten, don't give up on wisdom.

The second conclusion is this: "The words of the wise heard in quiet are better than the shouting of a ruler among fools" (Eccl. 9:17). Pragmatically speaking there is effectiveness in a loud king, but what ultimately wins the day is wisdom without bluster. "Noisy popularity," said Charles Bridges, "has its influence for a moment. But the real and solid good are the words that are heard in quiet."[155] It is frustrating when people reject wisdom, but the alternative can never be loud rhetoric. Anyone can persuade a fool. Anyone can turn up the volume. Stay the course of wisdom.

The third conclusion is "Wisdom is better than weapons of war, but one sinner destroys much good" (9:18). The story of the small town and the hero reaffirms that wisdom is better than weapons, which are examples of power and strength. However, all it takes to undo the good done by wisdom is one single sinner. Maybe it is the loud, shouting ruler. Maybe it is the bungler. Maybe it is the angry guy, the bully, or the bonehead. All of this anticipates the coming chapter, but the point is clear: a fool can do a lot of damage and undo much good.

Life is full of frustrations, unmet expectations, and unexpected events. Even when good things happen, they are not appreciated. Even when a hero arises, no one cares. Instead, ingratitude wins the day. And although wisdom is better than strength, at the end of the day, all it takes is one rotten person to undo all the good. Life is full of these kinds

---

[155] Bridges, *Ecclesiastes*, 232.

of disappointments and unexpected events. We work hard. We do our best. We have expectations of the way things are going to go, and then it falls apart. Something else happens. We try to be wise, we try to do the right thing, and nobody notices. This is life. It is painful. But there are some things to remember:

1. Do not give up on wisdom because of the folly of others.

2. Do not give up doing the right things, in parenting, in marriage, in work, in your community, or your nation.

3. We cannot allow disappointments to derail us – wisdom is still better than strength, no matter what fools may do. Although other alternatives, such as becoming a cynic, or just looking out for number one, may be more appealing, disappointments are also vapors.

In trying to be wise and do our best, in the middle of the unexpected, in the midst of disappointments, in trying to serve others, only to experience ingratitude and sin, in the middle of sacrifice and then being forgotten, remember this: there was a poor wise man who delivered not a town but the world. That wise Man is the Son of God, who became the Savior of the world. Such wisdom and grace! And yet what ingratitude! How He is forgotten and ignored, marginalized, and mocked. But He stayed the course for our good. We can stay the course for His glory. Remember the Man of Sorrows. See Him, who rejected and despised, set His face like flint toward Jerusalem for our rescue (Isa. 50:7). Despite all the evil opposition, He endured (Heb. 12:1–3). So do not give up on hard work and wisdom. Sometimes God does great and awesome things which we did not expect (Isa. 64:3). Keep your hand to the plough.

16

The Lives of the
Wise and Foolish
(10:1–20)

A re you a wise person? Or are you a foolish person? Not many would willingly claim the latter. But this world is littered with fools. Wisdom of course, is from God. The fear of the Lord is the beginning of wisdom (Prov. 1:7; 9:10). The wise person knows God, he walks with God, and trusts His Word. As one Old Testament scholar put it, "The presupposition of all wisdom is the fear of God. In other words ... relationship precedes ethics."[156] *Who* I know comes before *how* I live. *How* I live flows out of *who* I know. This wisdom "is the ability to navigate life well."[157] Wisdom is skill in how to live, how to speak, and how to relate to others. This wisdom comes from knowing God.

The fool lacks the knowledge of God. He does not know God personally. Therefore, the fool lacks the ability to navigate life well. The fool's moral compass cannot locate true north because there is no fear of God in his heart or before his eyes. The fool is a disaster in his relationships and a trainwreck in his words. The fool is on a path where his folly will grow worse and the opportunities to become wise diminish. The path of the fool ends in catastrophe. Wisdom and folly are matters of life and death.

---

[156] Raymond B. Dillard and Tremper Longman, *An Introduction to the Old Testament* (Grand Rapids: Zondervan, 1994), 238.

[157] Tremper Longman, *How to Read the Proverbs* (Downers Grove: IVP, 2002), 13.

In Ecclesiastes 9, Solomon dealt with unexpected events and disappointments in life. In chapter 10, Solomon arranges some proverbs on wisdom and folly. His arrangements paint two portraits, the wise and the fool. The purpose of the portraits is to get us to look in the mirror of God's Word and identify ourselves with honesty. This is not an easy thing for us to do. We do not like to be criticized or have our sins exposed. Our pride stands in the way of looking honestly at the portrait. But if we would live wisely, we need an accurate self-assessment. We need an objective gaze at the portrait.

The Weight of Folly (10:1)

> [1] Dead flies make the perfumer's ointment give off a stench; so a little folly outweighs wisdom and honor.

This verse is connected to 9:18, which said, "One sinner destroys much good." Little flies drop into the vat of the perfumer's oil and drown in aromatic bliss. The flies are literally "flies of death." Although tiny, the "flies of death" make the perfume stink. One little fly that drops into the aromatic oil can nullify both the beauty and appeal of the perfume. The conclusion is simple: a little foolishness is weightier than wisdom and honor. This proverb can be taken two ways. Perhaps both are intended. The first is that a man's wisdom and honor can be unraveled by one sinner (9:18). Through slander, gossip, lies, innuendos, and verbal attacks, a good man's character can be ruined. The second view is a man's character, wisdom, and honor, have a pleasant fragrance. Yet small mistakes, small indiscretions, small acts of foolishness, can outweigh an overall good character. Derek Kidner notes, "It takes far less to ruin something than to create it.… There are endless instances of prizes forfeited and good beginnings marred in a single reckless moment."[158] Think of Israel's great King David. When our minds go to the man after God's heart, we may think of him slaying the giant, but we may also just as easily think of David's notorious

---

[158] Kidner, *The Message of Ecclesiastes*, 88.

sins nearly slaying him. A life of overall faithfulness and courage stained with one large blot.

This should put the wise man on notice. The folly that is so abundant in a fool may only have small traces in the wise man's heart yet it is even more dangerous. "The unguarded moment— the hasty word—the irritable temper—the rudeness of manner— the occasional slip—the supposed harmless eccentricities—all tend to spoil the fragrance of the ointment."[159]

The Way of Folly (10:2–3)

> [2] A wise man's heart inclines him to the right, but a fool's heart to the left.
>
> [3] Even when the fool walks on the road, he lacks sense, and he says to everyone that he is a fool.

The right hand is the place of power, protection, blessing, strength, and even salvation (e.g., Gen. 48:13–14; Ps. 16:8; Isa. 41:10; Matt. 25:33–34). The left hand was never viewed so positively. In fact, our word "sinister" comes from the Latin word for "left hand." The left-hand lacks skill, strength, and dexterity. The left hand is the place of damnation, not salvation (Matt. 25:33, 41). The wise man is inclined to strength and blessing. The fool has no such inclination. In truth, he is inclined to the opposite. The whole tenor of the fool's life is exposed; it is self-evident. His choices leave nothing to the imagination. He is as predictable as they come.

Folly is a heart problem. The fool takes no counsel. He scorns advice. He chooses the path of least resistance. As he refuses to listen to wisdom, his folly is on display for everyone to see. All the fool must do to be exposed as a fool is "walk along the road." Whether "walk along the road" is a metaphor for just living life or literally just engaging in a journey on a marked path, the point is clear: "His heart is lacking."[160] This expression has nothing to do

---

[159] Bridges, *Ecclesiastes*, 234, italics original.

[160] I've given a literal translation. Most English versions have something like "his sense is lacking" (NASB) or "he lacks sense" (ESV, NIV).

with lacking courage or emotion. Rather the heart is the center of the mental and emotional faculty and thus the seat of wisdom. The fool lacks heart in that he lacks a heart for wisdom and thus a heart for God. He lacks a heart that loves the truth and hates error. He lacks a heart that has godly priorities and deep convictions. Therefore, he has no understanding.

The Reign of Folly (10:4–7)

> [4] If the anger of the ruler rises against you, do not leave your place, for calmness will lay great offenses to rest.
>
> [5] There is an evil that I have seen under the sun, as it were an error proceeding from the ruler:
>
> [6] folly is set in many high places, and the rich sit in a low place.
>
> [7] I have seen slaves on horses, and princes walking on the ground like slaves.

A ruler may get angry with a wise man. The ruler may be a king, a governor, or just a superior. The tendency is to cave in under such pressure. But Qoheleth counsels to hold your position with composure. There is no virtue in being a "yes man." Daniel exemplified this wisdom in Babylon. He served within a corrupt system, but he served with integrity and in truth. Calmness under such circumstances can help to mitigate the perceived offense and may even open the ruler's ear.

A ruler may promote a fool. This is an error, and it is evil. Folly is set in an exalted place, while the rich (successful men of resources) sit in places of humility. The damage is lasting. Appointing people who are incompetent simply because they are a supporter or fit some desired demographic is terrible folly. Such folly turns the world upside down. From Solomon's perspective, an upside-down world looked like slaves riding horses and princes walking like slaves. Everything seems equal! The ninety-nine percent are now the one percent. Democracy at its finest. But in an upside-down society, those who have knowledge and understanding, those who have wisdom and insight, are marginalized and replaced with fools.

The halls of government are occupied by those who have never read the Constitution. They have no sense of history or sacred traditions. I remember many years ago during the presidential primaries I commented on a candidate that I liked. My dad's response was that "he will never win. He is too smart." This is not simply a political issue; it is a moral issue.

The Cost of Doing Business (10:8–11)

> [8] He who digs a pit will fall into it, and a serpent will bite him who breaks through a wall.
>
> [9] He who quarries stones is hurt by them, and he who splits logs is endangered by them.
>
> [10] If the iron is blunt, and one does not sharpen the edge, he must use more strength, but wisdom helps one to succeed.
>
> [11] If the serpent bites before it is charmed, there is no advantage to the charmer.

Pits, serpents, quarrying stones, splitting logs, dull axes, and don't forget, snake charmers are next on the list. Folly and wisdom are contrasted by the themes of risks, dangers, successes, and failures. Failure to use wisdom and old-fashioned common sense may result in serious injury. You may put an eye out! "Use wisdom in your daily work and avoid getting hurt."[161]

Qoheleth's counsel here is simple. Apply wisdom to your daily tasks, make preparations, take precautions, and you will live longer. For example, change the oil in your car, back up your hard drive, use your turn signal before you change lanes, and look both ways before you cross the street. Especially for the men, do not stack one ladder on top of two ladders so that you can get higher to hang the Christmas lights.

---

[161] Sidney Greidanus, *Preaching Christ from Ecclesiastes* (Grand Rapids: Eerdmans, 2010), 244.

Know the risks of the job you are about to do and take reasonable measures to avoid injury or death.

The last picture in the passage may be only slightly familiar to many of us. It is the snake charmer. He charms snakes for a living. A cobra is in a basket, the lid is taken off, the flute is played, the snake is charmed, so people are amazed and throw a few bucks in his tin cup. If the skilled snake charmer carelessly removes the lid, or doesn't pay adequate attention, the snake may bite him before he can charm the snake. Show over. Not only does he not make any money, but he also probably falls over dead.

The Weariness of Folly (10:12–15)

> [12] The words of a wise man's mouth win him favor, but the lips of a fool consume him.
>
> [13] The beginning of the words of his mouth is foolishness, and the end of his talk is evil madness.
>
> [14] A fool multiplies words, though no man knows what is to be, and who can tell him what will be after him?
>
> [15] The toil of a fool wearies him, for he does not know the way to the city.

When it comes to the use of our words, the book of Proverbs is a veritable handbook, with dozens of proverbs dealing with what comes out of our mouths. Words are vital. Proverbs 18:21 tells us the sobering truth, "Death and life are in the power of the tongue, and those who love it will eat its fruits." There is a lethal power to our words that can cut, wound, and kill (Prov. 12:18; James 3:5–6; Eph. 4:29). There is a life-giving power to our words. Good speech is a tree of life (Prov. 11:30; 15:4). Good speech is a fountain of life (13:14). Wise words bring healing (12:18; 16:24). Gentle words turn away wrath (15:1). Good and wise words can cheer, strengthen, and edify. Whether our words are words of death or words of life, there is a cord that goes from our hearts straight to our tongues. The two organs are connected. Our Lord Jesus tells us, "For out of the abundance of the heart the mouth speaks" (Matt. 12:34). Indeed, the mouth is one of the most accurate gauges of the heart's wisdom or folly.

The wise man's words in Ecclesiastes 10:11 "are gracious in content, winsome in spirit, affectionate in appeal, and compliant and affable in tone."[162] How hard this is for some of us! There is no social virtue in being a person who just says what is on our minds. We may think that we are just being a "straight shooter," but restraint and grace are more often the need of the moment than our snap judgments and sharp words (Eph. 4:29).

"The lips of the fool consume him." The fool's words are not simply destructive, they are *self*-destructive. His words get him into trouble, his words hurt others, and his words destroy himself. The fool's speech goes from folly to wicked madness. The New Jerusalem Bible translates Ecclesiastes 10:13 like this: "His words have their origin in stupidity and their ending in treacherous folly." Despite this, the fool continues to multiply his words. The fool knows that he doesn't really have anything to say, but he says it anyway. To make his point, which doesn't exist to begin with, he uses bravado and bold assertions, while he is racing toward insanity. "Words are too often a substitute for thinking, rather than a medium of thought."[163] The fool spouts off about not only what he does not know but what he cannot know.

Verse 15 seems to indicate that through the fool's endless talking, he wears himself out. That he wears out those around him is a given. The phrase "he doesn't know the way to the city" could be a reference to the utter stupidity of the fool much like the modern expression "that boy could get lost on an escalator."[164] Or it could be further reference to the folly of the fool's speech. His blathering is so profuse that he cannot even give simple directions to town.

---

[162] Kaiser, *Ecclesiastes*, 110.
[163] Bridges, *Ecclesiastes*, 251.
[164] Wilson, *Joy at the End of the Tether*, 109.

The Government of Folly (10:16–17)

> [16] Woe to you, O land, when your king is a child,
> and your princes feast in the morning!
>
> [17] Happy are you, O land, when your king is the son
> of the nobility,
> and your princes feast at the proper time,
> for strength, and not for drunkenness!

No stranger to national and international politics, Qoheleth observes that there is a curse on the land when it is led by children, that is, childish, self-centered, and inexperienced adults. There is a curse on the land when it is led by politicians who see their position and privilege as personal advantage and a platform for their own pleasure. The notion of princes feasting in the morning has to do with gluttony and drunkenness (Isa. 5:11, 22–23).

On the contrary, the land is blessed when the king is of nobility. Those of nobility understand their responsibility and take it seriously. Noble leaders work during the day, eat at night, not for revelry, but for strength. "The prosperity of the land is traced back to the responsible behavior of those who rule over it."[165] Those who govern with self-control and discipline rather than self-indulgence and drunkenness bless their land and people.

Of Sloths and Good Things (10:18–19)

> [18] Through sloth the roof sinks in,
> and through indolence the house leaks.
>
> [19] Bread is made for laughter,
> and wine gladdens life,
> and money answers everything.

Laziness is simply irresponsible. It will always take a toll and do damage. The lazy will experience the slow judgment of decay, whether that is a sagging, leaky roof or any other area of life not properly attended to and maintained.

---

[165] Farmer, *Proverbs and Ecclesiastes*, 188.

Verse 19 presents a challenge. Some think it is a further illustration of a lazy life devoted to food, wine, and money. Although this is possible, Qoheleth has warned us against living for money and these three staples of life have been presented as God's gifts. It is very possible that the verse presents the opposite of the lazy life. Living a life of industry instead of sloth brings enjoyment to life (enjoyments which elude the lazy). Money is necessary for both good food and wine. Laziness brings a leaky roof, industry keeps nice food on the table, wine in the glass, and money in the account.

"Money answers everything" is not an absolute and is certainly an overstatement. Nevertheless, it is necessary to have some money if one is to enjoy the gifts of this vaporous life. This does not nullify the happy poor or the miserable rich, but if you have to choose to live with or without money, the choice is obvious (cf. 7:12).

My wife and I are by no means rich. But we remember what it was to scrape money together to go to the grocery store. On one occasion, early on in seminary, I took some valuable baseball cards to a sports shop to sell them so we could get groceries for that week. That was a long time ago. At the time of writing this chapter, I am on vacation with my family. Something we could have never done in those early days. I know what I prefer.

How Twitter Began (10:20)[166]

> [20] Even in your thoughts, do not curse the king,
>   nor in your bedroom curse the rich,
>   for a bird of the air will carry your voice,
>   or some winged creature tell the matter.

Qoheleth warns us to watch our words. Do not curse in secret. Do not curse the king. Do not curse a rich man. A little bird might make the matter known. The famous logo for Twitter is a little bird. Words imprudently spoken have a way of getting out. This applies to words typed on a keyboard too!

---

[166] Well, the little bird has disappeared and Twitter is now X.

An unkind word spoken in secret has the uncanny ability not to remain secret. Once those words are out, they are out, and they can become the fly in your ointment. They can fracture relationships; they can get you in hot water. Illustrations abound.

Conclusion

Portraits have been painted. The wise watch their words and their deeds. The wise take the path of strength and blessing. The wise calmly hold their position when they know they are right. They apply wisdom for greater success. They guard their mouths and speak gracious words. The wise man remembers that it is out of the abundance of the heart the mouth speaks (Matt. 12:34).

The fool on the other hand chooses the tantalizing path, the easy road. He lacks self-awareness and is oblivious to what is obvious to everyone else. The fool is lazy. He does not prepare for the tasks at hand. His words are his own undoing. He loves to hear himself talk and think everyone else does too. His laziness is seen as soon as you pull up to his house. It is seen in what they lack. The lazy man is a curse to his family, who also need to live under his sagging rafters.

It might be easy to conclude that Qoheleth just gave us some good old-fashioned common-sense advice. Although that is true, he did much more than that. In Scripture, wisdom and folly are not merely intellectual issues. They are moral and spiritual issues. Although the passage does not explicitly mention God, wisdom assumes the fear and knowledge of God (Prov. 1:7; 9:10). Choosing wisdom is not merely pragmatism, but it comes from a heart that knows God and wants to do his will. "Look carefully then how you walk, not as unwise but as wise, making the best use of the time, because the days are evil. Therefore, do not be foolish, but understand what the will of the Lord is" (Eph. 5:15–17).

In the end, wisdom and folly are matters of life and death. If one continues to be a fool, one will become hardened in their folly and in that state drifts into being a scoffer. Scoffers are rarely rescued. They rarely turn. They are too wise in their own eyes and believe their own "wisdom" is sufficient. This is the way of death (Prov. 12:14). Wisdom is a tree of life (3:13). Wisdom is personified in the person of Jesus Christ, who makes us wise unto salvation (2 Tim. 3:15), as well as wise in a world that in its own wisdom does not know God (1 Cor. 1:18–25).

The portraits are painted. Do you see yourself?

17

Solomon's Money Makeover Plan (11:1−6)

The Things of Earth

In chapters nine and fourteen I mentioned Joe Rigney's books, *The Things of Earth* and *Strangely Bright*. As we come to yet another passage that deals with money, I thought it might be helpful to set forth Rigney's thesis as a framework for this chapter.

As we read our Bibles, we frequently encounter two categories of passages. The first is what Rigney calls "totalizing passages."[167] These are passages that teach us to be supremely and completely devoted to God and that God is indeed everything. One example of a totalizing text would be "if then you have been raised with Christ, seek the things that are above, where Christ is, seated at the right hand of God. Set your minds on things that are above, not on things that are on earth" (Col. 3:1–2). Our union with Christ in His resurrection has set us on the pursuit of the things above, a pursuit of Christ Himself. Life in Christ is a life of fixing our minds on the things above, not the things that are on the earth. Jesus demands total devotion. He is to be sought above all else. He is the treasure that we seek. There are many passages like this one which make it clear that we have a higher calling, a heavenly one, which is where our eternal treasure is.

---

[167] Rigney, *Strangely Bright*, 15.

But there are other passages which Rigney calls "things of earth passages."[168] These passages teach us that God in His goodness has created everything and has given us those things for our enjoyment in this earthly life. One such passage, from Paul as well, is "as for the rich in this present age, charge them not to be haughty, nor to set their hopes on the uncertainty of riches, but on God, who richly provides us with everything to enjoy" (1 Tim. 6:17). This passage combines a totalizing theme, "put your hope in God, not money," with a things of earth theme, "who richly provides us with everything to enjoy." This theme of enjoying the gifts of God is in many other places in Scripture but has a unique place in Ecclesiastes. We are not to shun the good gifts, seeing them as only poison or snares.[169]

Rigney then helpfully shows us a way to approach these two kinds of passages. There is the comparative approach—what is greater? There is no question, God in Christ is greater, heavenly treasure is greater, and eternal glory is greater than any of the things of earth. But then there is the integrative approach—God and His gifts are enjoyed together. We are not to show disdain for the things of earth, since they too are gifts from God. They are simply lesser gifts. The lesser gifts point us to the greater gifts, and when we enjoy the lesser gifts as gifts, we can enjoy them for God's glory. The totalizing passages always stand ready to test our hearts for idolatry. As we said earlier, "Good gifts make bad gods." The totalizing texts expose our idolatry and keep the gift perspective in view.

Money as a Thing of Earth

Money is a big part of life. It is certainly one of the things of earth. As we have seen in Qoheleth, money can be at the center of all kinds of problems. It can easily become an idol that separates God from His gifts. Money can be a source of stress. There may be times when the lack of sufficient funds causes us tremendous anxiety. Wondering how we will pay rent

---

[168] Rigney, *Strangely Bright*, 16.
[169] See chapter 14.

can be massively stressful. Debt, either through our own doing or perhaps even outside of our control, can weigh heavily on us and keep us awake at night. There are numerous potential frustrations when it comes to money. We may focus too much on it (Qoheleth has warned us against that). We may ignore financial concerns, be lazy, and pay the price for it (Qoheleth has warned us against that too). There are two extremes to avoid. The first is we must avoid being so consumed with making money that wealth becomes an idol that devours us (Eccl. 4:5-8; 6:1-12). The other extreme is through laziness, or lack of prudence, we fall into poverty. Both wealth and poverty can cause sleepless nights.

What we need when it comes to money is wisdom. We need wisdom to use and enjoy this "thing of earth" called money. We need wisdom to know how to get it, how to use it, and how to enjoy it without loving it.[170] Solomon gives us some good counsel here for a financial fitness plan. He doesn't say everything there is to say, but he says enough to set us in the right direction.

Be Generous (11:1)

> [1] Cast your bread upon the waters, for you will find it after many days.

Commentators have wrestled with whether this is an exhortation to charity or to invest. Qoheleth could be saying, "Put your money out for the sake of others without expecting a return even though you know that a return will come." Or he could be saying, "Invest overseas." This second option is how the NIV takes it: "Ship your grain across the sea; after many days you may receive a return."[171] Both Fredericks and Farmer say it is simply a part of the "you don't know what the future will bring" motif.

---

[170] I heartily recommend Jim Newheiser's *Money, Debt, and Finances: Critical Questions and Answers* (Phillipsburg, NJ: P & R, 2021). Jim also has a 31 devotional on the same topic. See, *Money: Seeking God's Wisdom, 31-Day Devotionals for Life* (Phillipsburg, NJ: P & R, 2019).

[171] The NET ("Send your grain overseas, for after many days you will get a return.") and the NLT ("Send your grain across the seas, and in time, profits will flow back to you.") both translate like the NIV.

In my estimation the traditional view wins the day. Qoheleth is telling his audience to be generous without expecting reciprocation, and yet God one day will bring it back to you.

The Puritan, Thomas Gouge, exhorted his readers, "Christian charity, rightly performed, is the surest way to plenty and happiness, it being usually rewarded with temporal blessings here, as well as with eternity hereafter.… I dare challenge all the world to give me one instance, or at least any considerable number of instances of any truly merciful men, whose charity hath undone them.… A compassionate heart, and a helping hand, will gather much by distributing; such giving is getting; such bounty is the most compendious way to plenty."[172]

Diversify (11:2)

> [2] Give a portion to seven, or even to eight, for you know not what disaster may happen on earth.

Qoheleth's financial fitness plan moves from generosity to diversification. We don't know the future, so we shouldn't put all our eggs in one basket. There is wisdom in investing. Doing so puts the money God has given to us to work. But we should invest wisely. "Diversification might keep you from participating in spectacular returns in one particular type of investment, but it should help us protect you from major losses."[173] The principle is simple: spread the risk.

Some of us are inept in the world of finance and investment. That's OK. John Calvin didn't care about money either. But if we are going to be wise with the money God gives us, if we want to be wise about the future, then we may simply need to seek counsel and direction from a trusted friend who is more adept at these things.

---

[172] Thomas Gouge, *Riches Increased by Giving*, (Harrisonburg, VA: Sprinkle, reprint 1992), 42–44.
[173] Newheiser, *Money, Debt, and Finances*, 230.

Keep a Loose Grip (11:3)

> [3] If the clouds are full of rain, they empty themselves
> on the earth, and if a tree falls to the south or to the
> north, in the place where the tree falls, there it will
> lie.

Qoheleth is telling us that there is an uncertainty when it comes to this life, and we cannot bank on anything to turn out to our advantage. When dark clouds come rolling in, we expect rain. The rain may be a blessing because it waters the crops, but it may be a curse by bringing calamitous floods. Nobody knows what clouds full of rain will do, and nobody can do anything about it. When a tree falls, it may be a blessing and provide firewood to heat one's home. Or it could fall the other way and crush one's home. Where it lands is not determined by our best laid plans. Blessing or calamity may result. There is an uncertainty to life, and we do not know what will work to our advantage or disadvantage. The application is to keep a loose grip and not cling to anything too tightly. Be generous. Be prudent. Be realistic; nothing is certain.

Work Anyway (11:4)

> [4] He who observes the wind will not sow, and he who
> regards the clouds will not reap.

Because there is always uncertainty looming over us, we cannot procrastinate as we try to prognosticate. The picture is a farmer who is always waiting for the right circumstances to do his work. Perhaps the problem is that he is overly meticulous in his approach to work. Perhaps he is simply lazy. Either way, the farmer never sows and never reaps while he waits for the perfect circumstances.

Procrastination is a financial killer. "When it comes to work just hit it. Excuses are always plentiful. Too hot. Too cold. Too late."[174] Don't procrastinate when it comes to being generous.

---

[174] Wilson, *Joy at the End of the Tether*, 111.

Don't procrastinate when you know what to do. When it is time to sow, then sow. When it is time to reap, then reap. "The duty is ours; the results are God's."[175]

No Guarantees (11:5)

> [5] As you do not know the way the spirit comes to the bones in the womb of a woman with child, so you do not know the work of God who makes everything.

The ESV translates verse 5 as one mystery.[176] But the NASB, along with many other English versions, translates it so that two mysteries are in view. "Just as you do not know the path of the wind and how bones *are formed* in the womb of the pregnant woman, so you do not know the activity of God who makes all things" (11:5 NASB). One of the challenges is the ambiguity of the word *ruach*, which can mean, "breath, wind, spirit." Qoheleth may be saying we do not know the way of the wind, or the way of the spirit, or the way of the spirit in the bones of a womb, or how the spirit comes to the bones in the womb. Although we should not be dogmatic, it seems that in context, the unpredictability of the wind (11:4) may well carry over into this verse, so that *ruach* is a reference to the wind. We do not know where and when the wind will blow (cf. John 3:8). "Nor are the 'kicking' movements of the fetus's limbs in the womb predictable. Qoheleth's conclusion by analogy, then is that God's other activities are unpredictable as well."[177] We are ignorant of God's work.

Knowing that God is sovereign does not help us to know where or how much to invest. But knowing that God is sovereign does remind us that our lives and our money are ultimately in His hands, who governs the wind and forms babies in the secrecy

---

[175] Kaiser, *Coping with Change*, 176.

[176] The Tanakh also translates it as one mystery: "Just as you do not know how the life breath passes into the limbs within the womb of the pregnant woman, so you cannot foresee the actions of God, who causes all things to happen" (Eccl. 11:5 TNK). Likewise, the RSV says, "As you do not know how the spirit comes to the bones in the womb of a woman with child, so you do not know the work of God who makes everything."

[177] Fredericks, "Ecclesiastes," 235.

of a womb. So, "Do not boast about tomorrow, for you do not know what a day may bring" (Prov. 27:1).

Seize All Opportunities (11:6)

> ⁶ In the morning sow your seed, and at evening withhold not your hand, for you do not know which will prosper, this or that, or whether both alike will be good.

Qoheleth urges us to be diligent in our duties because we do not know the outcome. This note has been sounded throughout this section, which should remind us of the uncertainty of riches. Prosperity may result from one effort, or another, or both. But if no effort is made, no prosperity will ever come. Jim Newheiser counsels, "A person who needs work should spend as much time pursuing a job as he or she would spend working at a job. Many seeds might be sown before the harvest comes."[178] Wherever there is opportunity, seize it. When opportunities are few, diligently seek to create opportunities by expanding your skills, working on certifications, or furthering training. Hard work is godly. Doing what we can when we can and leaving the outcome in the hands of God is the only way to live.

Conclusion

In this brief section, Qoheleth addresses money matters. He has urged us to be generous. This is the first principle! Give without knowing exactly what will come back, but know that God will bring it back to you in His time. Start your financial fitness plan by being a giver. Be wise and diversify. There are many uncertainties, so work hard and trust God. God has given money for us to enjoy (1 Tim. 6:17), so the wise pursuit and use of it honors God. Money as one of His many gifts requires wisdom, and it requires us to know that we cannot serve God and money (Matt. 6:24). Money is one of the things of earth. It cannot satisfy. Only Christ is the eternal treasure who truly satisfies our hearts.

---

[178] Newheiser, *Money, Debt, and Finances*, 95.

18

Don't Waste the Prime of Life
(11:7–10)

Youth and the prime of life are gifts from God. But we go out of our way to spoil both gifts. Derek Kidner has astutely observed, "To idolize the state of youth and to dread the loss of it are disastrous: it spoils the gift even while we have it."[179] Our culture is obsessed with looking young. We do everything we can to keep it, prolong it, or just pretend we still have it. People spend untold amounts of money on looking young—creams, lotions, pills, injections, suctions, you name it. One look at our culture and you may conclude that the only people who really matter are thin, attractive, and between twenty to thirty-five or so. If you fall outside of that age bracket, do your utmost to make yourself look like you fit. Paul Tripp calls this trend the "cult of youth."[180]

Qoheleth is going to do what Qoheleth does. He is going to give us perspective which enables us to enjoy the gift without idolizing and spoiling it. If you are young, listen to Solomon carefully! If you are past the prime of life, listen to Solomon carefully! Solomon is going to show us how to enjoy the

---

[179] Kidner, *The Message of Ecclesiastes*, 99.
[180] Paul Tripp, "Appearance is Everything? Reclaiming God's Image in an Image Obsessed Culture" *The Journal of Biblical Counseling* 23.4 (2005): 35-37.

prime of life responsibly and prepare for old age gracefully. If we take this small section seriously, we will avoid the "cult of youth" without diminishing the joy of youth. If we take this section to heart, then we will look to old age with a sense of realism that enhances the enjoyment of every year that God gives us to "see the sun."

Live in the Light (11:7)

> ⁷ Light is sweet, and it is pleasant for the eyes to see the sun.

I love the mornings. When my wife and I go on a road trip, we leave while it is still dark. There is this almost magical feeling that comes upon me as the eastern sky starts to show signs of light. As the darkness recedes, the light gets brighter, and then the sun appears. It is wonderful. Perhaps even better than the sun coming up during a road trip is the experience of first light on a hunt. We leave when it is cold and dark. But it is morning, not night. The promise of the dawn brings anticipation. When the sun finally breaks on the horizon, it is beautiful. When the sun comes up, it brings warmth and light. It makes you glad to be alive. Qoheleth uses the nearly magical quality of the sun to speak of the wonder, blessing, and joy of this life.

Life is full of clouds and rain, and at times, enshrouded with darkness (11:8). But there is also light. "How sweet the light!" The light symbolizes the joy of life. As the sun rises, bringing with it light and warmth, there is deep satisfaction in the start of a new day. It is the best part of the day. This is yet another use of the word "good" to convey "pleasant, sweet, enjoyable." Because the light is sweet, it is good to enjoy life. Solomon's point is simple. We won't always experience the pleasantness of the light of life; there will indeed be dark days. And the older we get, the dark days increase. So it's a blessing to see the light while we can.

Enjoy Your Years (11:8)

> [8] So if a person lives many years, let him rejoice in them all; but let him remember that the days of darkness will be many. All that comes is vanity.

Qoheleth underscores the call to enjoyment in verse 8. Sometimes God gives people a long life. One member of our church, Bob Edwards, was given nearly 102 years. That seems like such a long time. But remember the perspective. Whether God gives us 102 years or only 19, life is still a breath. But if God gives many years in this short vaporous life, Qoheleth says we should enjoy all of them. Enjoy every short vaporous chapter in this short vaporous life. We don't get to turn back the page, let alone the chapter, so enjoy the page while you are on that page and enjoy each chapter as you are in that chapter.

Recently I was looking through some old computer files, and I found a file of videos taken back in 2008. About half of them are of my son Alex's baseball games. In almost every baseball video I can hear my dear friend Arne Digerud cheering for Alex. Arne rarely missed a game. Arne went home to be with Jesus in 2021. I can hear my other son Zach, cheering for his brother in his fourteen-year-old voice, which hadn't changed yet. One video has eleven-year-old Alex hitting a grand slam. Sweet, but past. I'll never hear *those* voices again. I'll never see those sights again. If all I do is look at old pictures and watch old videos and mourn and pine for those days, then I spoil the current chapter. Qoheleth's wisdom is life-changing. Enjoy each chapter while you are in it. Enjoy each year while you have it, and don't try to cling to it and relive it. Don't spoil the gift because it is past.

We must remember we won't always be able to experience the warmth of the sun and the sweetness of its light. So it is good to see it while you can because it won't always be there. The aging process will bring limitations and restrictions to what we are able to do and able to enjoy. Vigor gives way to ailments.

Ailments give way to death. Qoheleth is not trying to depress us. Rather he is pressing on us the urgency of enjoying life right now. Qoheleth's counsel is to give full commitment to a sanctified *carpe diem*, seize the day. Seize the joy. Seize it for God's glory. Seize it while you have it. Seize it before old age comes.

Then Qoheleth tells us all that comes is *hebel*, that is, vapor. So the prime of life is a breath. Old age is a breath. It is all a breath. The days of light are a breath. The dark days of old age are a breath. The older we get the faster the vapors disappear. The people who enjoy life best are the ones who know they won't always be able to enjoy it like they do now.

Enjoy Your Youth (11:9)

> [9] Rejoice, O young man, in your youth, and let your heart cheer you in the days of your youth. Walk in the ways of your heart and the sight of your eyes. But know that for all these things God will bring you into judgment.

"Youth" is both the time and quality of being young. The NASB's "childhood" is too restrictive. The NET captures it well: "You who are young, be happy while you are young." The NIV translates it like this: "You who are young, be happy while you are young." The NLT says, "Young people, it's wonderful to be young." If you are a young person, know this, it is wonderful to be young. Those wonderful, short years are a gift from God, and God commands us to rejoice in them. "Let you heart cheer you in the days of your youth." Let those days give you joy.

Again, it is a divine imperative that demonstrates being young is a gift from God. The days go by so quickly, but they are days that should be enjoyed. Imagine! God is telling young people to make sure they enjoy the youth He has given them and maximize the joy of the prime of life.

The next part of the verse can be scary, especially depending on your translation and especially if you are the parents of teenagers! The NASB says, "Follow the impulses of your heart and the desires of your eyes." For parents of kids heading to college, this is not exactly what they want their teens to hear! This is not a license for hedonism. It is a call to live your youth to the full. The call here is not to sensual pleasure. Solomon has already shown us that living for pleasure is a bust (Eccl. 2). To "walk in the way of your mind and the sight of your eyes" is to experience the enjoyments and achievements of youth as they are new and fresh to our taste. When we are young, we gain new perspectives, experience new things, and they are wonderful. There is a time when we give up our preference for mac-and-cheese over steak. There is that day when we look at someone for the first time and think we are in love (we are probably wrong, but it's a nice feeling). All of these things and so many more constitute these wonder years.

There is of course a qualifier for any who want to push the envelope. "But know that for all these things, God will bring you into judgment." Qoheleth says, "Now don't forget, you will give an account for how you enjoyed the gift of youth." Enjoy the gifts of God; don't abuse them. Abusing God's gifts results in idolatry and idolatry results in judgment. God will judge on how we either abused God's gifts or enjoyed them. This qualifier is not only a reminder for the morally flexible but also for the morally uptight. The promiscuous break God's command and will be judged. The sullen and sour, whose biggest fear is that they might be having fun, will also be judged. Those who sacrifice divinely commanded joy for their own phony piety are just as bad as those who color way outside the lines. Both abuse the gift of God.

Walter Kaiser reflects this balance when he says, "Life must be lived with eternity's values in view. Your one life will soon be past, and only what is done for Christ and with eyes fixed on

Christ will last. So have fun! Rejoice and delight yourself in the thrill of living."[181]

Too Short to Waste (11:10)

> [10] Remove vexation from your heart, and put away pain from your body, for youth and the dawn of life are vanity.

The word the ESV translates "vexation" (*ka'as*) in Hebrew means to be angry, or grieved, or provoked to wrath. The word has a wide range of meanings, reflected in the variety of words used in the translations. "Sorrow" and "anger" are common translations. The NET uses "emotional stress," while the NASB includes both ideas: "Remove grief and anger from your heart."[182] Of course we cannot always avoid grief, but perhaps Qoheleth is telling us to put away the stuff in our life that eats up our life and consumes our joy. I can't control grief or sadness when it comes, but I can make sure that I put off anger and anxiety. There is nothing to be gained in being an angry person. The angry person has no capacity to look beyond their own irritations to see any good in life. Anger sucks the joy right out life. Life is truly too short to spend it in on anger, anxiety, or stress.

Then we are told to "put away pain from your body." Isn't this what Bengay is for? Or Advil? Qoheleth is not talking about the aches and pains of old age. The word has a moral connotation. The Hebrew word *ra'ah* also has a wide range, but "evil and misery" are in view here. Garrett rightly says, "Not personal sin here but the trouble and evil that is part and parcel of human life."[183] The miseries and troubles of this life are many. Qoheleth

---

[181] Kaiser, *Ecclesiastes*, 117. Kaiser echoes the last line of C. T. Studd's famous poem, "Only One Life." It read, "Only one life, 'twill soon be past, Only what's done for Christ will last." For this poem, see "Only one Life, Twill Soon Be Past—by C. T. Studd (1860–1931)," https://reasonsforhopejesus.com/only-one-life-twill-soon-be-past-by-c-t-studd-1860-1931/.

[182] The Greek Old Testament (LXX) uses *thumon*, which is anger or wrath.

[183] Garrett, *Proverbs, Ecclesiastes, Song of Songs*, 340, n. 226.

urges us to put away as much of it as we can. There is so much in this life that can consume us, so much to fret over, and so much to be distressed over or angry at. Qoheleth says these things can cripple us and consume us, so put them away. We must seek to be free from the injuries and miseries that threaten to steal our joy.

Qoheleth concludes this section with "youth and the dawn of life are vanity." The ESV's "dawn of life" is a translation for "black hair." "Black hair" is a metaphor for the prime of life before the gray hair comes. This short chapter of life is fleeting. What a reminder. Our lives are vapors, a mere breath. Our choices in youth can become the foundation for a wise and happy life, or they can mold us into fools. Youth (and dark hair) is a gift from God. Don't waste it. Enjoy it as God's gift. Live it as one who will stand before God.

Because these short years are a gift from God, soak in the sunlight, taste its sweetness, revel in new experiences, including love and the wife of your youth. Don't delay. The sun is setting, and it will not wait for you. The light will fade. Live life to the full. God requires it of you. But live it remembering your Creator (12:1). Come to Christ when you are young. Very few turn to Him when they are old. Jesus will not ruin your life; He will save you and redeem your youth. He will give you joy and perspective that will last a lifetime and all eternity. In Him, you will never waste this breath.

19

When the Gifts Slip Away
(12:1–8)

Old Age: The Unexpected Gift

If you really want to live, stand by a graveside. If you want to really enjoy life, go to a funeral. Take in the sights, the sounds, the tears, and the joys at the funeral and then ponder your own. Contemplate the graveside, with all its finality for this life. Consider that one day your loved ones and friends will stand around your graveside. Living life in view of the end is the best way to embrace it as a gift.

But what about the process that leads to the grave? What about growing old? Someone once said, "It is not death that scares me, it is the thought of dying that scares me." David Gibson writes, "Growing old …. leaves a person depressed at the disconnect between the mirror and the mind."[184] We joke about getting old, but there comes a point when the jokes aren't funny anymore. So if life is a gift, and we dare not waste the prime of life, then what do we make of the aging process? What do we make of old age?

First, old age is when the gifts of this life start to slip away. It is sad. There is loss. The gifts we once enjoyed now slip through our fingers, as we lose our grip on them. As we increasingly lose our

---

[184] Gibson, *Living Life Backwards*, 132.

grip, those gifts appear to be lost. But this too is a gift. How so? Back in chapter seventeen we talked about (1) totalizing texts and (2) things of earth texts.

Totalizing texts are texts which teach complete devotion to God and that God is everything (Pss. 16:11b; 73:25–26; Phil. 1:21; Col. 3:1–2). He is all in all. He is supreme. He is the greatest treasure and chief joy. Both "things of earth" texts or "life is a gift to be enjoyed" texts teach us that God in His goodness has created everything and given us the things of earth to enjoy. As Paul says, "Instruct those who are rich in this present world not to be conceited or to fix their hope on the uncertainty of riches, but on God, *who richly supplies us with all things to enjoy*" (1 Tim. 6:17, emphasis added). And Jesus said, "If you then, who are evil, know how to give good gifts to your children, *how much more will your Father who is in heaven give good things to those who ask him!*" (Matt. 7:11, emphasis added).

We then said, drawing from Joe Rigney's insights, that we can compare these texts and also integrate these texts. When we compare these the totalizing texts with the things of earth texts, there is no comparison. "To live is Christ" is supreme. "Seek first his kingdom and his righteousness," is greater than anything on earth or any temporary gift. But the integrative approach says God and His gifts are enjoyed together. God is enjoyed through His gifts. In this life, we don't have to despise the gifts that God gives us. I don't have to hate marriage because I love Jesus supremely. Rather, marriage is all the sweeter because I love Jesus supremely. I love and delight in the gift because I love and delight in the Giver.

If old age is when the gifts start to slip away, how is that a gift? As the things of earth start to slip away, we see how important those totalizing texts are. In other words, as the temporary gifts start to fade, the eternal Gift shines even more brightly. As the things of earth grow dim, we begin to experience the reality and nearness of the eternal more acutely.

Joe Rigney asks,

> What will we do when we are faced with the loss of
> *all* good things? What will we do when the reality
> of death lands on us, the reality that we and all
> the created delights we love are vapor, breath,
> fading grass? What will we say and do when we
> are about to lose the created beams of glory that
> warm our hearts and bring us joy? … Integrated
> delight in God's gifts knows that Christ is the joy
> of all our joys, the pleasure at the heart of every
> pleasure, and that death simply opens up new
> vistas for knowing and enjoying him.[185]

As we grow old and get closer to heaven, our love to God
begins to take on new dimensions, new contours, new colors,
new anticipations. Old age is a gift because it forces us to ask
ourselves, "When the gifts slip away, do we still love the Giver
supremely? Do we love Him more than ever and long to finally
be with the One who gave us all good things to enjoy?" Old
age, like little else, exposes the heart. As the gifts slip away, one
is exposed as either an idolater or a lover of God. Old age can
bring us closer to God or it can be very dangerous!

Before Qoheleth gets there, he has his parting word to
the young.

Remember Your Creator (12:1)

> [1] Remember also your Creator in the days of your
> youth, before the evil days come and the years draw
> near of which you will say, "I have no pleasure in
> them."

The world's message for young people is simple: forget God!
Sin is fun; God is boring. Forget God; you are just a cosmic
accident. Forget God; you are god. Forget God; be your own
god. Be the captain of your ship, the master of your fate. What a
lie! What an illusion.

---

[185] Rigney, *The Things of Earth*, 226.

Qoheleth's message is remember your Creator. Notice, it is not simply to "remember your God" but to "remember your Creator." Remember the One who made all things. Remember the One who made the world good. Remember the One who made you, who gave you good things to enjoy, and to whom you are accountable.

Young people are reminded: you have a Creator. He formed you in your mother's womb (Ps. 139:13–16). He made you in His image (Gen. 1:27). Because you bear your Creator's image, you have dignity, you have a moral compass, and you have a sense of justice and eternity written on the heart. The unbeliever resents being made in the image of God, and as much as he may try to hide it or bury it, he can't. The image is like an albatross around his neck, and wherever he goes, there it is. You are something more than matter in motion. You are made in the image of your Creator.

He is your Lawgiver (Eccl. 12:13). On tablets of stone and on your own heart, He has written the rules and standards for life. The Creator establishes the rules. We don't get to make up our own rules. We have a Creator who is also the lawgiver. When we try to be a law unto ourselves, we have a conscience that reminds us that it just isn't so. And He will be your Judge (12:14). He is the one to whom we will give an account.

When Qoheleth calls the young to "remember," it is a call to reflect, embrace, and act.

"Remember" in the Bible is more than to mentally recall something. It is to reflect in a way that produces action. If I say to my wife, "Remember that restaurant on the River Walk in San Antonio?" all I am asking is if she has a recollection of a place or an event.

To remember in the Bible is more like the saying "Remember the Alamo." After Santa Ana's army of 6,000 had laid siege to the old mission and then decimated 187 Texian defenders, Sam Houston's army gave no quarter and descended upon the napping Mexican army at San Jacinto with shouts of "Remember the Alamo!"

The shout to "remember" was a rallying cry to motivate courageous action. It passionately called to mind the massacre, but it was more than mere recollection. It was a call to action.

The call to remember your Creator is certainly a call to reflection, but it is more than that. It is an urgent call to respond to your Creator and to respond decisively. The time to remember is in the days of your youth. Why not wait until one is old? Because God deserves the prime of our life; He deserves our youth. Furthermore, youth is also the time in which we are most formative and pliable. The miracle of the new birth is always a miracle, but youth is free from decades of resistance and rebellion. Youth does not have the moral and intellectual baggage of old age. Conversion in old age is rare compared to those who turn to God in their youth. Remember your Creator "before the evil days come and you say I have no delight in them." In other words, remember in your youth before you are old.

Old age is described as "evil days" because they can be distressing with infirmities. They are often dark days without much sunshine. The gifts have started to slip away and the challenges of old begin to increase. Archibald Alexander vividly describes this painful process: "Where is the bloom of youth, the robust strength of manhood, the eye sparkling with intelligence, and the countenance beaming with animation? Alas! They are fled; and in their place we see the decrepit body, the sunken eye, the withered countenance, and the tottering gait."[186]

Qoheleth urges, remember your Creator before these days come! "To forget the Creator of youth is to invite bitter regrets and an empty existence in old age. To remember the Creator is to follow the path of wisdom and extend the joy of life."[187]

Now Qoheleth gives some vivid, if not somewhat cryptic, descriptions of old age.

---

[186] Archibald Alexander, *Thoughts on Religious Experience* (Edinburgh: Banner of Truth, 1989), 266.

[187] Garrett, *Proverbs, Ecclesiastes, Song of Songs*, 341.

Vivid Descriptions of Old Age (12:2–5)

[2] before the sun and the light and the moon and the stars are darkened and the clouds return after the rain,

[3] in the day when the keepers of the house tremble, and the strong men are bent, and the grinders cease because they are few, and those who look through the windows are dimmed,

[4] and the doors on the street are shut—when the sound of the grinding is low, and one rises up at the sound of a bird, and all the daughters of song are brought low—

[5] they are afraid also of what is high, and terrors are in the way; the almond tree blossoms, the grasshopper drags itself along, and desire fails, because man is going to his eternal home, and the mourners go about the streets—

"Remember ... before the sun and the light, and the moon and the stars darkened, and the clouds return after the rain" (12:2).

The capacity to enjoy life is diminishing. The ability to bounce back after physical setbacks dramatically decreases. During our youth if we encountered a rainstorm, we knew the sun would come out again (figuratively speaking). We knew we would recover. We were confident that normal life would return. But in old age, instead of the sun coming out after a rainstorm, it is only followed by more clouds. In youth, sickness passes, health returns. In old age, one rain cloud is followed by another, sorrow after sorrow, sickness after sickness. Barry Davis explains the succession of clouds as "the repetitive gloom into which the elderly may be prone to fall as they encounter setback after setback in the final years of their lives."[188]

---

[188] Barry C. Davis, "Death, An Impetus for Life" (Eccl. 12:1–8), in *Reflecting with Solomon*, ed. Roy Zuck (Eugene, OR: Wipf & Stock, 2003), 356.

"In the day when the keepers of the house tremble" (12:3).

The watchmen of the house are the arms and hands. The arms and the hands, once strong and sturdy, now shake with age. A few months ago, my wife and I went to visit a member of our church who was declining. As we walked into his room at the rehab hospital, I was saddened at how weak and frail he looked. Tom was once a mighty man. His arms were strong from years of work. But as he sat there in a wheelchair, those mighty keepers of the house shook with weakness. A painful reminder that old age is coming.

"The strong men are bent" (12:3).

The NASB's "mighty men stoop" is more vivid. The mighty men are probably the legs, now weakened and bent with age. The once upright and confident gait is now bent with the wear and tear of relentless years.

"The grinders cease because they are few" (12:3).

The tooth population is declining, and the remaining survivors are less active.

"Those who look through the windows are dimmed" (12:3).

The eyes lose their strength in old age. Our eyes simply get old. It is called "presbyopia." This is not a Presbyterian disease! But the word is related. *Presbyteros* is "elder." "Presbyopia is the gradual loss of your eyes' ability to focus on nearby objects. It's a natural, often annoying part of aging. Presbyopia usually becomes noticeable in your early to mid-40s and continues to worsen until around age 65."[189] Then after that we can look forward to glaucoma, cataracts, or macular degeneration.

"The doors on the street are shut—when the sound of the grinding is low" (12:4).

The imagery here is debated. It could possibly symbolize the loss of hearing. The doors are the ears which are now shut, and one can barely hear the grinding sound produced at the mill.

---

[189] For details on Presbyopia, see Mayo Clinic, "Presbyopia," https://www.mayoclinic.org/diseases-conditions/presbyopia/symptoms-causes/syc-20363328.

Or, as others have suggested, the lips curling over gums, while one eats soft food. Neither are appealing.

"One rises up at the sound of a bird" (12:4).

The picture here is despite loss of hearing, the aged one is a light sleeper, awakening even at the tiny sound of a bird chirping.

"All the daughters of song are brought low—" (12:4).

Although a bird chirping wakes them up, they can no longer hear and thus appreciate music and song.

"They are afraid also of what is high, and terrors are in the way" (12:5).

The NASB says, "Furthermore, men are afraid of a high place and of terrors on the road." No more ladders, no more escalators, no more stairs. The elderly become increasingly afraid to travel. The elderly want to stay home or get back home as quickly as possible.

I saw this with my grandfather. My grandpa Herb raised pigs for as long as I can remember. If they were visiting on a Saturday, he would say at some point, late in the afternoon, "Bea, we need to go, I gotta feed the pigs." That was true for years. But then one Saturday I heard him say, "We gotta go, I need to feed the pigs." But he didn't have any more pigs. He simply wanted to get home before it got dark. The elderly want to stay away from anything that poses a threat, such as driving at night.

"The almond tree blossoms" (12:5).

White hair overtakes the once black hair of the prime of life.

"The grasshopper drags itself along" (12:5).

This picture is especially challenging. Walter Kaiser says it "describes the halting gait of the elderly as they walk along with their canes."[190]

"Desires fail" (12:5).

The NASB is more faithful, but a little more ambiguous: "And the caperberry is ineffective." Many commentators believe that

---

[190] Kaiser, *Ecclesiastes*, 121.

the caperberry was an aphrodisiac that aroused sexual desire and power. The image then is being impotent. The lack of sexual desire cannot be reversed with ancient or modern caperberries.

"Because man is going to his eternal home, and the mourners go about the streets—" (12:5).

Old age culminates in death. Man "goes to his eternal home." The mourners are out in the street, perhaps the family, just recently gathered around the deathbed, are now conversing with each other in the kitchen and the front porch. Death has come and taken another victim. The body which was deteriorating had finally given out. Don't miss the echo for the young. Old age is coming, death is coming. Remember your Creator now! Remember Him long before death knocks at your door.

Vivid Descriptions of Death (12:6–7)

These anatomical puzzles are more difficult than the pictures of old age. So challenging are these following images that some commentators avoid specific descriptions and say something like Daniel Fredericks: "The imagery of an ended life is brutal and final: life is removed, smashed, broken, and crushed."[191] Others, like Walt Kaiser, take a good stab at specific meanings. We will suggest the meanings of each metaphor, with some reservation.

> [6] before the silver cord is snapped, or the golden bowl
> is broken, or the pitcher is shattered at the fountain,
> or the wheel broken at the cistern,
>
> [7] and the dust returns to the earth as it was, and the
> spirit returns to God who gave it.

"Before the silver cord is snapped, or the golden bowl is broken" (12:6).

The NASB helps connect this to context with *"Remember Him before the silver cord is broken and the golden bowl is crushed."* Some think this is a reference to the spine (the silver cord) and the brain (the golden bowl). The point is that they no longer function; they no longer do what they are supposed to do.

---

[191] Fredericks, "Ecclesiastes," 239.

"The pitcher is shattered at the fountain" (12:6).

The Puritan William Bridge suggested it was the bladder "which did hold the urine, which in old age doth insensibly pass away."[192] Others see it as the heart failing.

"The wheel broken at the cistern" (12:6).

This could be the failure of the pulmonary system or the nervous system.

Whatever these allegorical images may represent, the point is clear: that which functioned at one time, served a purpose at one time, and was beneficial at one time, is now gone, crushed, shattered, and worthless. The body has finally given in to death. The ravages of old age, which are a precursor to our death, are often cruel and unrelenting.

"And the dust returns to the earth as it was, and the spirit returns to God who gave it" (12:7).

What's interesting is that as Qoheleth describes old age and its ravages, which end in death, he uses obscure metaphors and images. But when he really focuses on death, he speaks unambiguously. He speaks in terms of the curse. In a book infused with Genesis 3, Qoheleth reminds us that these bodies came from dust and will return to dust, as God told Adam, "For you are dust, and to dust you shall return" (Gen. 3:19). In Adam we all sinned, and in Adam we all die (Rom. 5:12).

Solomon does not leave us disintegrating back into the earth. He says, "And the spirit will return to God who gave it" (Eccl. 12:7). He has already noted that "man goes to his eternal home" (12:5b). Although not a thorough perspective on the afterlife, it is an affirmation that the soul/spirit is separated from the body at death and returns to the God who gave it. Even though these bodies wind down and finally give out, Solomon tells us that is not all there is. Our lives don't end when the dust returns to dust. Once our eyelids close in death, there is still life.

---

[192] William Bridge, "A Word to the Aged," in *The Works of William Bridge* (Edinburgh: The Banner of Truth Trust, 2022), 5:182.

And it is that knowledge that keeps us sane when a loved one leaves us in death. To know that the spirit returns to God who gave it gives us hope and gives us peace. The grave does not have the last word! Jesus who conquered death has the last word! "Since therefore the children share in flesh and blood, he himself likewise partook of the same things, that through death he might destroy the one who has the power of death, that is, the devil" (Heb. 2:14).

The Verdict on Old Age and Death (12:8)

[8] Vanity of vanities, says the Preacher; all is vanity.

Or in keeping with our exposition, "Breath of breaths, says Qoheleth; everything is breath" (12:8). Qoheleth finishes with how he started (1:2). Vapor of vapors, everything is a vapor—everything is temporary! Youth is a vapor. Old age is a vapor. Life is a vapor. This life, which is a gift, will be over before we know it.

The only way to enjoy this life is (1) see it as a gift, not an achievement; and (2) see it as a vapor! Live it from the standpoint of the deathbed. As the gifts begin to slip away, realize how blessed you were to have had them for as long as you did. As Vin Scully, the famed baseball announcer of sixty-seven baseball seasons, said on his retirement, "Don't cry because it's over. Smile because it happened."[193]

The Dangers of Old Age

Old age can be a dangerous time. These are "evil days." The Puritan William Bridge, in "A Word to the Aged," reminds his readers that there are not only physical infirmities that hinder old age, but there are also moral infirmities. He notes, the elderly are apt to be too covetous and tenacious for the things of the world. "As wantonness is the young man's vice, so covetousness is the old man's sin."[194] He says, they are apt to be too fearful. "They are apt to be too touchy, peevish, angry and forward,

---

[193] The source of this quote is disputed with Dr. Seuss being the likely source.
[194] Bridge, "A Word to the Aged," 182.

for old age is a continued sickness, and in sickness men are apt to be angry."[195] They might think they know more than others and become unteachable. They become hard to please, full of complaints. "Apt are they also, to think and speak of the sins of their youth with delight, and so to commit them again by thought and word which they cannot come at by their action."[196]

Bridge counsels his older readers to "be sure that you do not chew the cud of your former sins, by musing on them with delight, for thereby you justify your former practice; but rather mourn over them, for the way to keep from future sins is to mourn for former; and the way to be kept from sins of old age, is to mourn for the sins of our youth."[197] He also observes that they can become suspicious, always suspecting and fearing the worst. The dangers of old age are very real.

Old age will test our commitments to totalizing texts as the things of this earth grow strangely dim. If there is much resentment and even anger at old age, it is because we are coveting our younger years. We spoil the gift of youth by grasping it too tightly. The truth is it is gone, and it is not coming back. But for those who have walked with God and have their affections on Christ, they enjoyed the gifts when they had them, and now they look forward to something greater. Joe Rigney is again insightful, "Death takes away our earthly delights, and the resurrection restores them in spades. Nothing good will ever be finally lost. It's not just that all the best joys here point to joys there, but that many of the best joys here will actually be there, only glorified, transfigured, and heightened beyond our imagination."[198]

The Unicorn in *The Last Battle* says it well: "I have come home at last! This is my real country! I belong here. This is the land I have been looking for my whole life, though I never knew it until now. The reason why we loved the old Narnia is that it

---

[195] Bridge, "A Word to the Aged," 182.
[196] Bridge, "A Word to the Aged," 183.
[197] Bridge, "A Word to the Aged," 184.
[198] Rigney, *The Things of Earth*, 227.

sometimes looked a little like this. Bree-hee-hee! Come further up, come further in."[199]

So as you age, as the gifts slip away, look to God for growing-old grace. When I am an old man, I don't want to be a cranky, grouchy old man. I want to be the kind of old man who is full of grace and wisdom. I want my grandchildren and greatgrandchildren to want to be around me because of that grace and wisdom. I want them to enjoy great stories from me, and even better, I want them to listen with joy as I testify to God's faithfulness to me all the days of my life. When they gather around my deathbed, if God gives me one, I want their faith to be strengthened because I am confident and excited to go see Jesus. I want their memories of me to point them to my God and Savior.

As we come to our last breath, look to God for dying grace. We may think of that day with fear and trepidation. We may wonder how we will handle standing on the edge of eternity. God will give you all the grace you need, but only when you actually need it. He won't give you a measure of it on Monday and expect you to ration it until Friday. The God of all grace will meet you with dying grace, sustaining your faith, so that you cross the river on firm ground.

So be ready for tomorrow by taking care of your relationship with God today. Make sure your walk with Jesus is strong. Make sure you are grounded in His Word. Be filled with the promises of God. Have your eyes fixed on the future. Then, when you come to die, you will have nothing to do but to die.[200]

---

[199] Lewis, *The Last Battle*, 213.
[200] Bridge, "A Word to the Aged," 190.

20

When All Is Said and Done
(12:9–14)

We have come to the end of the ride. There have been bumps, jolts, hard turns, and even a whiplash or two. But the ride was worth it. The lessons learned and the perspectives gained are invaluable. Now we come to the grand conclusion, and Qoheleth is going to tie the threads together. Qoheleth is going to describe his calling, talk about the nature and source of his words, and give us the conclusion which applies to every person.

Qoheleth's Calling (12:9–10)

> [9] Besides being wise, the Preacher also taught the people knowledge, weighing and studying and arranging many proverbs with great care.
>
> [10] The Preacher sought to find words of delight, and uprightly he wrote words of truth.

Qoheleth is clearly a sage, a wise man. His wisdom is inspired, biblical wisdom. Let me reiterate that if Solomon's message was that everything was meaningless, that nothing matters, then how could he possibly claim that he is a wise man teaching others wisdom? "He taught people knowledge" (12:9). Qoheleth is the master teacher. He has observed and studied God and life in the crucible of daily realism. If everything is vanity, if it is all futility, then what knowledge could he have possibly imparted? Knowledge and truth presuppose meaning. So again, the message is not that life is meaningless but that it is vapor.

Qoheleth "weighed and studied and arranged many proverbs with great care" (12:9). The word "weighed" (ESV) is "pondered" in the NASB. It could be translated "listened intently." He listened of course to God, but he also listened to the world around him, and he listened to others. Qoheleth is the student before he is the teacher. This touches on the reason why Qoheleth's relevance hits us like a freight train: he is asking the questions we ask, and he is wrestling with the issues we wrestle with. Furthermore, "he searched out and arranged many proverbs." He gathered from the best, the brightest, and he adapted and arranged a collection of proverbs. This book of Ecclesiastes is a book of wisdom.

Qoheleth also "sought to find words of delight" (12:10). The words he sought were pleasing. As Daniel Fredericks notes, these are "not comfortable words of recreational reading. They are not the ear-tickling words that placate the soul superficially or soothe the conscience artificially. Instead, the delightful aspects of these words are in their expressions of the truth about life and God."[201] Qoheleth has set the truth in front of us in a way that, although at times painful, strikes home, resonates, makes sense of our lives, and gives a satisfying perspective. Qoheleth wanted people to enjoy his words not just because he was a wordsmith but because he told the truth.

The book continues and says of Qoheleth that "uprightly he wrote words of truth" (12:10). He wrote the words of truth correctly. Those who claim that Qoheleth is a foil, or unorthodox, or just says stuff that isn't true, need to reckon with this claim. In Qoheleth's studies, pondering, and searching, his goal was to put forth words of truth, written with beauty and accuracy. This wasn't spiritual fast food; it was thoughtfully prepared meals of wisdom and knowledge. Beauty and truth!

---

[201] Fredericks, "Ecclesiastes," 247.

Qoheleth not only wanted the truth to be seen, but to be tasted and appreciated for its beauty.

Words of Delight Given by One Shepherd (12:11–12)

> [11] The words of the wise are like goads, and like nails firmly fixed are the collected sayings; they are given by one Shepherd.

> [12] My son, beware of anything beyond these. Of making many books there is no end, and much study is a weariness of the flesh.

The words of the wise are like goads.[202] A goad was a sturdy stick with a sharpened end. It was used like a cattle prod. Qoheleth says the words of the wise are a stimulus, a prod, a poke, that moves us in the right direction. Getting poked with a sharp stick is usually no fun, but sometimes necessary for the stubborn. But then Qoheleth says, "Like nails firmly fixed are the collected sayings." The NET puts it like this: "The words of the sages are like prods, and the collected sayings are like firmly fixed nails" (12:11). What are these well-driven nails? They could be a picture of stability and strength. But the Tanak better captures the metaphor by saying, "Like nails fixed in a prodding stick." The words of the wise are like prods, and when they are collected, they are like nails fixed in the prodding stick. Getting poked with a sharp stick is one thing, but having some nails fixed on it provides quite a bit of extra motivation. The words of the wise are not always a carrot on a stick but a few nails in a sharp stick.

The words are given by one Shepherd. The one Shepherd is the Lord himself. He gives the words of wisdom, and he uses those of wisdom like a cattle prod for his foolish, stubborn, erring children. So once more, we need to see these words of wisdom in Ecclesiastes are given to us not by a secularist or

---

[202] In addition to the words of the wise being goads, they also "bring healing" (Prov. 12:18b), are a "fountain of life" (13:14), make "knowledge acceptable" (15:2), and "spread knowledge" (15:7). As a result, there is a duty: "Incline your ear, and hear the words of the wise, and apply your heart to my knowledge" (22:17).

a cynic but by our Good Shepherd. This epilogue is where all the negative views of Ecclesiastes come to die. This is God's wisdom for God's people. It is not earthly wisdom, although it is certainly earthy. It is not a picture of life without God. It is gritty and real life under the rule of God.

The next sentence is very difficult. It reads, "My son, beware of anything beyond these" (12:10). These words are probably a warning meaning, "In addition, my son, pay close attention to these things." Qoheleth, as a wise father, is giving a closing exhortation to pay close attention to the words of wisdom and make them a priority. The next line helps us and says, "Of making many books there is no end" (12:10). The connection between the two lines is clear. Pay attention to the inspired words of wisdom given by one Shepherd. Make them a priority because the stream of uninspired books is an endless stream.

The next line brings cheers from all the kids. It says, "Much study is a weariness of the flesh." Yay! Too much studying is bad for my health. Solomon says so! Well not exactly. In light of the whole book, Qoheleth is saying God has given you inspired wisdom—master that! Books that try to explain the meaning of life are all from uninspired philosophies, and they never end. There is a sufficient Word, and it is not nature; it is divine revelation. As Spurgeon famously put it: "Read the books, by all means, but especially the parchments. Search human literature, if you will, but especially stand fast by that Book which is infallible, the revelation of our Lord and Savior Jesus Christ."[203]

The Conclusion Which Applies to All (12:13–14)

> [13] The end of the matter; all has been heard. Fear God and keep his commandments, for this is the whole duty of man.
>
> [14] For God will bring every deed into judgment, with every secret thing, whether good or evil.

[203] Charles H. Spurgeon, "Paul—His Cloak and His Books" (sermon presented at Metropolitan Tabernacle, London, 29 November 1863), 7. See also "Paul—His Cloak and His Books," https://www.spurgeongems.org/sermon/chs542.pdf.

The NASB's rendering here is preferable and says, "The conclusion, when all has been heard: fear God and keep his commandments."[204] Once His wisdom has been heard and hopefully received, then the conclusion of the matter is clear. Once the case has been made, once the journey has been complete, the summation of all of it is obvious. It is important to see that Qoheleth is not putting some addendum to his teaching like this: "Well, guys, I've droned on about life without God and the meaninglessness of it all, so let me say something spiritual: fear God and keep his commandments." Rather, Qoheleth's grand conclusion is the logical conclusion and necessary application of everything he has said in the whole book.

What does it mean to fear God and keep His commandments, and how do these two ideas relate? They relate since "fear God" and "keep his commandments" are two sides of the same coin. The fear of God is the beginning of wisdom (Prov. 1:7; 9:10; Eccl. 3:14; 5:7; 7:18; 8:12). The beginning of wisdom is not like the training wheels of wisdom that are left behind when you learn to balance. "The fear of the Lord is the beginning in that it is the first principle that pervades all other principles."[205] The fear of the Lord is the beginning of wisdom like the ABCs are the beginning of reading. Before you can read you need to learn the alphabet, but once you learn to read you rely on the alphabet for the ability to continue to read. Or as John Murray put it, "The fear of God is the soul of godliness."[206]

"Keep his commandments" is the other side of the coin to fearing God. In other words, to fear God is to obey His Word. As Solomon said elsewhere, "He who walks in his uprightness fears the LORD" (Prov. 14:2 NASB). And again, "A wise man is cautious and turns away from evil" (14:16 NASB).

---

[204] See also the NIV: "Now all has been heard; here is the conclusion of the matter: Fear God and keep his commandments" (12:13).

[205] Derek Kidner, *An Introduction to Wisdom Literature: The Wisdom of Proverbs, Job & Ecclesiastes* (Downers Grove: IVP, 1985), 17.

[206] John Murray, *Principles of Conduct: Aspects of Biblical Ethics* (Grand Rapids: Eerdmans, 1957), 229.

When I was a student in seminary, Dr. Bruce Ware gave us this definition of the fear of the Lord. This definition shows the relationship between fear and obedience: "To fear the Lord means to *tremble* before him because of the holiness of his character and his just judgment against all wickedness: and to *trust* him unreservedly because of the bounty of his goodness, mercy and blessing toward those who turn to him alone for their life and well-being-expressing itself in (1) a resolved and fervent opposition to all unrighteousness and wickedness, and (2) a *resolved and fervent* obedience to God's law, in humble recognition of God's rightful authority over our lives, for his glory and our good."[207]

Here is our anchor in the mist: fear God and obey His commandments. Obey His call to enjoy this fleeting life. Obey His call to trust Him. Obey His call to submit to Him in all humility. Obey His call to receive this short breath of a life as a gift. Keep in mind His majesty, His sovereignty, His mercy, His might, His holiness. Your anchor in the mist is the character of God, even when what He is doing is veiled with mystery.

The last line is disputed. In the ESV it reads, "This is the whole duty of man" (12:13). The NASB, on the other hand, reads, "This applies to every person." The NKJV comes closest to the Hebrew, saying, "This is man's all." Although the particulars may vary, the point is clear that everyone is held to this standard. No matter who you are, no matter what you say you believe, you have a Creator (12:1) who is holy and the King. This King is to be trusted, feared, and obeyed. This applies to everyone, at all times. It is the whole duty of every human being.

The reason it applies to all is because "God will bring every deed into judgment, with every secret thing, whether good or evil" (12:14). On that last and great day, no one will get off on a technicality. No one will slip through a loophole because of a slick attorney. There will not be one thought or one word

---

[207] Bruce Ware, Class Notes. Theology I. Western Seminary, Portland, Oregon, 1990, italics original.

that will escape the One who judges with perfect knowledge of all our thoughts, feelings, words, motives, and deeds. This judgment was already mentioned in Ecclesiastes 3:17 and 11:9 and is the consistent testimony of Scripture: "And no creature is hidden from his sight, but all are naked and exposed to the eyes of him to whom we must give account" (Heb. 4:13).

Such knowledge does not inhibit our joy. It simply reminds us of the bigger picture. Life is short. It is God's gift. We are accountable.

Conclusion

As the book closes, when all is said and done, look to Christ who is our Good Shepherd, our wisdom, and our righteousness. Look to Christ who is our chief joy and greatest treasure.

Do not waste this short, fleeting life. Seize every opportunity to obey God by enjoying this life for His glory, living for the Great Shepherd of the sheep, marveling at His gifts, both the temporary ones and the eternal ones. This is what God requires of you.

Epilogue

We still go to the Oregon coast every summer. In fact, we go to the same little town. Now my wife and I go with our grown kids and their kids. At times I still say, "Where has the time gone?" But that question gives way to this: we are here today, enjoying the beauty of the ocean, in one of our favorite spots in the world, with our favorite people. This is a gift from God today. Enjoy it today. It is a breath; don't waste it.

Bibliography

(*Commentaries which deal with *hebel* as breath, vapor, or mist, or are at least sympathetic to the view).

Alexander, Archibald. *Thoughts on Religious Experience.* Edinburgh: Banner of Truth Trust, 1989.

Alexander, T. Desmond and Brian Rosner, eds. *New Dictionary of Biblical Theology.* Downers Grove, IL: InterVarsity Press, 2000.

Allen, Ronald B. "Seize the Moment, Meaning in Qohelet." Paper presented at the Northwest Section Meeting of the ETS. Portland, OR. April 1988.

Archer, Gleason. *A Survey of Old Testament Introduction*, Revised ed.Chicago: Moody Press, 1974.

Bauer, Walter, William F. Arndt, Wilbur Gingrich, and Frederick W. Danker, eds. *A Greek-English Lexicon of the New Testament and Other Early Christian Literature.* 3rd ed. Chicago: University of Chicago Press, 2000.

Bavinck, Herman. *Holy Spirit, Church, and New Creation.* Vol. 4 of *Reformed Dogmatics.* Edited by John Bolt. Translated by John Vriend. Grand Rapids: Baker Academic, 2008.

Beale, G.K. *A New Testament Biblical Theology: The Unfolding of the Old Testament in the New.* Grand Rapids: Baker Academic, 2011.

Black, Hugh. *The Art of Being a Good Friend.* Manchester, NH: Heritage, 2019.

Borgman, Brian. Review of *Breaking the Idols of Your Heart* in *SBJT* 12.1 (2008) 116–18.

Bridge, William. "A Word to the Aged." Pages 179–96 in vol. 5 of *The Works of William Bridge*. Edinburgh: The Banner of Truth Trust, 2022.

Bridges, Charles. *Ecclesiastes*. Geneva Series of Commentaries. Edinburgh: Banner of Truth Trust, 1992.

Brindle, Wayne. "Righteousness and Wickedness in Ecclesiastes 7:15 18." Pages 301–14 in *Reflecting with Solomon: Selected Studies on the Book of Ecclesiastes*. Edited by Roy B. Zuck. Eugene, OR: Wipf & Stock, 2003.

Currid, John D. Ecclesiastes: *A Quest for Meaning*. Leyland, England: Evangelical, 2016.

Dahl, Gordon. *Work, Play, and Worship in a Leisure-Oriented Society*. Minneapolis: Augsburg, 1972.

Davis, Barry C., "Death, An Impetus for Life" (Eccl. 12:1–8). Pages 347–66 in *Reflecting with Solomon*, ed. Roy Zuck. Eugene, Oregon, Wipf & Stock, 2003.

Dillard, Raymond B., and Tremper Longman, *An Introduction to the Old Testament*. Grand Rapids: Zondervan, 1994.

Eaton, Michael A. *Ecclesiastes: An Introduction and Commentary*. Vol. 18 of *Tyndale Old Testament Commentaries*. Downers Grove, IL: InterVarsity Press, 1983.

Edwards, Jonathan. *The Works of Jonathan Edwards*. Edinburgh: Banner of Truth Trust, 1990.

*Farmer, Kathleen. *Proverbs and Ecclesiastes: Who Knows What Is Good?* International Theological Commentary. Grand Rapids: Eerdmans, 1991.

Fee, Gordon and Douglas Stuart. *How to Read the Bible for All It's Worth*. 2nd ed. Grand Rapids: Zondervan, 1993.

Fox, Michael V. *A Time to Tear Down and a Time to Build Up: A Rereading of Ecclesiastes*. Grand Rapids: Eerdmans, 1999.

*Fredericks, Daniel C. *Coping with Transience: Ecclesiastes on Brevity in Life*. Sheffield: JSOT, 1993.

*_____. and Daniel J. Estes. *Ecclesiastes and The Song of Songs*. Vol. 16 of *Apollos Old Testament Commentary*. Downers Grove, IL: InterVarsity Press, 2010.

Garrett, Duane A. *Proverbs, Ecclesiastes, Song of Songs*. Vol. 14 of *The New American Commentary*. Nashville: Broadman & Holman, 1993.

Gentry, Kenneth. *God Gave Wine*. Lincoln, CA: Oakdown, 2001.

*Gibson, David. *Living Life Backwards: How Ecclesiastes Teaches Us to Live in Light of the End*. Wheaton, IL: Crossway, 2017.

Gouge, Thomas. *Riches Increased by Giving*, Reprint. Harrisonburg, VA: Sprinkle Publication, 1992.

Greidanus, Sidney. *Preaching Christ from Ecclesiastes*. Grand Rapids: Eerdmans, 2010.

Harris, R. Laird, Gleason L. Archer Jr., Bruce K. Waltke, eds. *Theological Wordbook of the Old Testament*. Chicago: Moody Press, 1999.

Henry, Matthew. *Matthew Henry's Commentary on the Whole Bible: Complete and Unabridged in One Volume*. Peabody: Hendrickson, 1994.

Holmstedt, Robert D., John A. Cook, and Phillip S. Marshall, *Qoheleth: A Handbook on the Hebrew Text*. Baylor Handbook on the Hebrew Bible. Waco, TX: Baylor University Press, 2017.

*Kaiser, Walter. *Coping with Change: Ecclesiastes*. Ross-Shire, Scotland: Christian Focus, 2013.

*_____. *Ecclesiastes: Total Life*. Chicago: Moody Press, 1979.

Keller, Timothy. *Ministries of Mercy*. Philipsburg: P & R, 1997.

Kidner, Derek. *The Message of Ecclesiastes: The Bible Speaks Today*. Downers Grove, IL: InterVarsity Press, 1976.

_____. *An Introduction to Wisdom Literature: The Wisdom of Proverbs, Job & Ecclesiastes.* Downers Grove, IL: InterVarsity Press, 1985.

Kline, M.M. "Is *Qoheleth* Unorthodox?: A Review Article," https:/kerux.com/doc/1303R1.asp.

Lewis, C.S. *The Last Battle.* New York: Harper Trophy, 1956.

Longman, Tremper and Dan Allender. *Breaking the Idols of Your Heart.* Downers Grove, IL: Zondervan, 2007.

Longman, Tremper. *How to Read the Proverbs.* Downers Grove: InterVarsity Press, 2002.

_____. *The Book of Ecclesiastes,* The New International Commentary on the Old Testament. Grand Rapids: Eerdmans, 1997.

Marsden, George. *Jonathan Edwards: A Life.* New Haven, CT: Yale University Press, 2003.

*Meyers, Jeffrey. *A Table in the Mist: Ecclesiastes Through New Eyes.* Monroe, LA: Athanasius, 2006.

Murray, John. *Principles of Conduct: Aspects of Biblical Ethics.* Grand Rapids: Eerdmans, 1957.

Newheiser, James. *Money, Debt, and Finances: Critical Questions and Answers.* Phillipsburg, NJ: P & R Publishing, 2021.

_____. *Money: Seeking God's Wisdom.* 31-Day Devotionals for Life. Phillipsburg, NJ: P & R, 2019.

*Ogden, Graham. *Qoheleth.* 2nd ed. Sheffield, Phoenix, 2007.

"Only One Life, Twill Soon Be Past—by C. T. Studd (1860–1931)." https://reasonsforhopejesus.com/only-one-life-twill-soon-be-past-by-c-t-studd-1860-1931/.

Piper, John. *Desiring God.* Colorado Springs, CO: Multnomah Books, 2011.

Poole, Matthew. *Annotations upon the Holy Bible.* Vol. 2. New York: Robert Carter and Brothers, 1853.

Provan, Iain. *The NIV Application Commentary: Ecclesiastes, Song of Songs*. Grand Rapids: Zondervan, 2001.

Rigney, Joe. *Strangely Bright: Can You Love God and Enjoy This World?* (Wheaton, IL: Crossway, 2020).

_____. *The Things of Earth: Treasuring God by Enjoying His Gifts*. Wheaton, IL: Crossway, 2015.

Risner, Vaneetha. "What if the Worst Happens." *Desiring God*. 15 September 2014. https://www.desiringgod.org/articles/what-if-the-worst-happens.

Sproul, R.C. *Not a Chance: The Myth of Chance in Modern Science and Cosmology*. Grands Rapids, Baker, 1994.

Spurgeon, Charles H. "Paul—His Cloak and His Books." Sermon presented at Metropolitan Tabernacle. London, 29 November 1863.

Steele, Richard. *A Remedy for Wandering Thoughts in Worship*. Harrisonburg, VA: Sprinkle, 1988.

Thomas, Derek. "Ecclesiastes 4: The Quandary of Oppression." Sermon given at First Presbyterian Church. Jackson, MS, 6 July 2003.

Tripp, Paul. "Appearance is Everything? Reclaiming God's Image in an Image Obsessed Culture." *The Journal of Biblical Counseling*, 23.4 (2005): 35–43.

Van Gemeren, Willem, General Editor. *New International Dictionary of Old Testament Theology and Exegesis*. Grand Rapids: Zondervan, 1997.

Vincent, Nathaniel. *Attending Upon God with Distraction*. Grand Rapids: Soli Deo Gloria, 2010.

Ware, Bruce. Class Notes. Theology I. Western Seminary, Portland, Oregon, 1990.

*Webb, Barry. *Five Festal Garments: Christian Reflections on The Song of Songs, Ruth, Lamentations, Ecclesiastes, and Esther*, NSBT. Downers Grove, IL: InterVarsity Press, 2000.

*Wilson, Douglas. *Joy at the End of the Tether: The Inscrutable Wisdom of Ecclesiastes*. Moscow, ID: Canon, 1999.

Wright, J. Stafford. "The Interpretation of Ecclesiastes" Pages 17 30 in *Reflecting with Solomon: Studies on the Book of Ecclesiastes*. Edited by Roy B. Zuck. Eugene, OR: Wipf & Stock, 2003.

Zuck, Roy, ed. *Reflecting with Solomon: Studies on the Book of Ecclesiastes*. Eugene, OR: Wipf & Stock, 2003. [There are some outstanding articles in this volume, see especially Ardel Caneday's "Qoheleth: Enigmatic Pessimist or Godly Sage?"].

Other Titles by Free Grace Press

Other Titles by Free Grace Press

Ten Essential Sermons of Charles Spurgeon by Charles Spurgeon

The Church by Jeffrey D. Johnson

The Crux of the Free Offer of the Gospel by Sam Waldron

The Exorcism of Satan by Joshua P. Howard

The Failure of Natural Theology by Jeffrey D. Johnson

The Gospel Made Clear to Children by Jennifer Adams

The Kingdom of God by Jeffrey D. Johnson

The Living Epistle by Cornelius Tyree

The Lust of the Flesh by Dr. Jared Moore

The Missionary Crisis by Paul Snider

The Story of Redemption by Jeffrey D. Johnson